MIKHAIL BARYSHNIKOV

CHARLES FRANCE

FOREGROUND: SUSAN JAFFE, LESLIE BROWNE, BARYSHNIKOV

BARYSHNIKOV AND OLGA EVREINOFF.
IN THE MIRROR: EVE ARNOLD AND JULIO BOCCA

MARTINE VAN HAMEL

LUCETTE KATERNDAHL AND JOHAN RENVALL
AFTER THE ANNUAL CHOREOGRAPHIC WORKSHOP PERFORMANCE

SUSAN JAFFE, LESLIE BROWNE, ALESSANDRA FERRI

BALLET STUDENTS WAITING FOR REHEARSAL

BARYSHNIKOV AND KATHLEEN MOORE REHEARSING FOR THE PREMIERE
OF MARK MORRIS'S *DRINK TO ME ONLY WITH THINE EYES*

Charles Dillingham

CHERYL YEAGER, JOHN TARAS, AMANDA MCKERROW

FLORENCE PETTAN

JULIE KENT

E LENA T CHERNICHOVA WORKING WITH A LESSANDRA F ERRI (*LEFT*) AND S USAN J AFFE

*PRIVATE
VIEW*

PRIVATE VIEW

*Inside Baryshnikov's
American Ballet Theatre*

JOHN FRASER

PHOTOGRAPHS
BY EVE ARNOLD

BANTAM BOOKS

TORONTO • NEW YORK • LONDON • SYDNEY • AUCKLAND

For my daughters,
Jessie, Kathleen, and Clara
J.F.

For Misha and the ABT
with affection and gratitude
E.A.

PRIVATE VIEW
A Bantam Book / December 1988

All rights reserved.
Copyright © 1988 by American Ballet Theatre and John Fraser.
Photographs copyright © 1988 Eve Arnold/Magnum.
Book design by Barbara N. Cohen.
No part of this book may be reproduced or transmitted
in any form or by any means, electronic or mechanical,
including photocopying, recording, or by any information
storage and retrieval system, without permission in
writing from the publisher.
For information address: Bantam Books.

Library of Congress Cataloging-in-Publication Data

Fraser, John, 1944–
  Private view.

  1. Baryshnikov, Mikhail, 1948–   2. Ballet
dancers—Russian S.F.S.R.   3. American Ballet Theatre.
I. Arnold, Eve, 1913–   II. Title.
GV1785.B348F73   1988   792.8'4'0924   [B]   88-47640
ISBN 0-553-05321-3
ISBN 0-553-05360-4

Published simultaneously in the United States and Canada

Bantam Books are published by Bantam Books, a division of Bantam Doubleday Dell Publishing Group, Inc. Its trademark, consisting of the words ''Bantam Books'' and the portrayal of a rooster, is Registered in U.S. Patent and Trademark Office and in other countries. Marca Registrada. Bantam Books, 666 Fifth Avenue, New York, New York 10103.

PRINTED IN THE UNITED STATES OF AMERICA

WAK   0 9 8 7 6 5 4 3 2 1

CONTENTS

ACKNOWLEDGMENTS

*I*n researching and writing this book, I am indebted first and foremost to Mikhail Baryshnikov and American Ballet Theatre. During a period of thirteen months, from August 1986 to September 1987, I trailed the elusive superstar and his company on both sides of the Atlantic. The snooping began in Bari, Italy, where the company was involved in a Herbert Ross film built around the classical ballet *Giselle.* During the ensuing year I camped out with the company in New York as it prepared for the coming season at its headquarters, and then later traveled with everyone as ABT toured America—to Los Angeles and San Francisco, to Chicago, back to New York for the annual season at the Metropolitan Opera House at Lincoln Center, and finally to Washington and the Kennedy Center. Everywhere I went I was allowed unlimited access: backstage and in the company's artistic offices and even at the annual meeting of the board of trustees. Sometimes I was around at moments of great internal stress or conflict, and only rarely was I asked to make myself scarce. Even then, it was not a question of trying to prevent my seeing or hearing what was going on—whatever was happening was always easy enough to discover afterward—but one of consideration for the privacy and dignity of a company member.

The degree of trust implicit in this unprecedented openness has often been daunting. It was a trust born of the hope that I would understand the temperament of a great ballet troupe, as well as the context for its frustrations and exhilaration. I have tried to repay that trust with a faithful depiction of the people and events I came up against during the course of researching and preparing *Private View.* I would be remiss, therefore, if I did not celebrate the sense of confidence and commitment that allowed Baryshnikov and ABT to concede such unfettered access to an interloper. My presence coincided with one of the most dramatic and emotionally charged years in the company's history, a year in which the challenge was not to embellish incidents in order to sustain the tale, but to keep the abundance of unexpected melodrama in some sort of perspective.

I owe more than the usual thanks to the editor-in-chief of Bantam Books, Stephen Rubin, for his unflagging enthusiasm for the project despite many setbacks, while the useful and always diplomatic suggestions of my editor, Beverly Lewis, were invaluable.

The Colbert Agency of Toronto, which has happily revolutionized the lives of writers in Canada over the past decade, played an important part in the writing of this book. Not the least of Nancy and Stanley Colbert's gifts was the offer of a quiet garret in which to do the actual writing. It would not have been completed otherwise.

Private View was researched and written during a period of personal transition which saw my life as a foreign correspondent in Europe for the Toronto *Globe and Mail* transformed into the editorship of Canada's oldest and most influential magazine, *Saturday Night.* At both institutions I was the beneficiary of considerable patience and cooperation: at the *Globe and Mail* from Editor-in-Chief Norman Webster and Managing Editor Geoffrey Stevens; at *Saturday Night* from Publisher Peter White and Senior Editor Barbara Moon.

I owe my own family the greatest debt. My wife, after coping with a transatlantic move following a grievous illness, was the personification of fortitude, and the resilience of my young daughters was a revelation.

I wish to acknowledge formally my gratitude to three great figures from the world of ballet who sustained me at different points of my career and who, for better or worse, bear responsibility for encouraging me. Betty Oliphant, the founder and principal of Toronto's National Ballet School, knows precisely the nature of my debt to her, a debt that has not changed one iota over the years. A decade and a half ago, Lincoln Kirstein at the New York City Ballet did not disdain the insistent demands for advice and criticism from a young provincial dance critic. Finally, the late Erik Bruhn, the former artistic director of the National Ballet of Canada, provided me with definitions of commitment and style in the ballet world which I still cling to with the fervor of a born-again believer. He is terribly missed by everyone who had the good fortune of knowing and enjoying his generous and broad affection.

The quotations attributed to Mikhail Baryshnikov in *Private View* are a faithful recounting of what he told me during numerous interviews and conversations over a period of fourteen months on two continents. Grammatically, however, the printed quotations are sometimes different from the spoken ones. Baryshnikov's English is lucid, forceful, and imaginative, but he is still learning the language. Having at first tried to render his words as they were actually spoken, and then having carefully examined the results, I realized that in print they did him a disservice. It seemed pointlessly condescending and counterproductive to serve up what still remains of his Russian-English patois. I tried to retain all the pungency of his strong opinions, but where there were grammatical errors, I have mostly cleaned them up, especially if he was making a serious, extended point. Baryshnikov's English has been learned on the run, and other efforts to serve up the dialect of earlier stages in his language development struck me as needlessly coy. As a result, I have avoided any such attempt.

PRIVATE VIEW

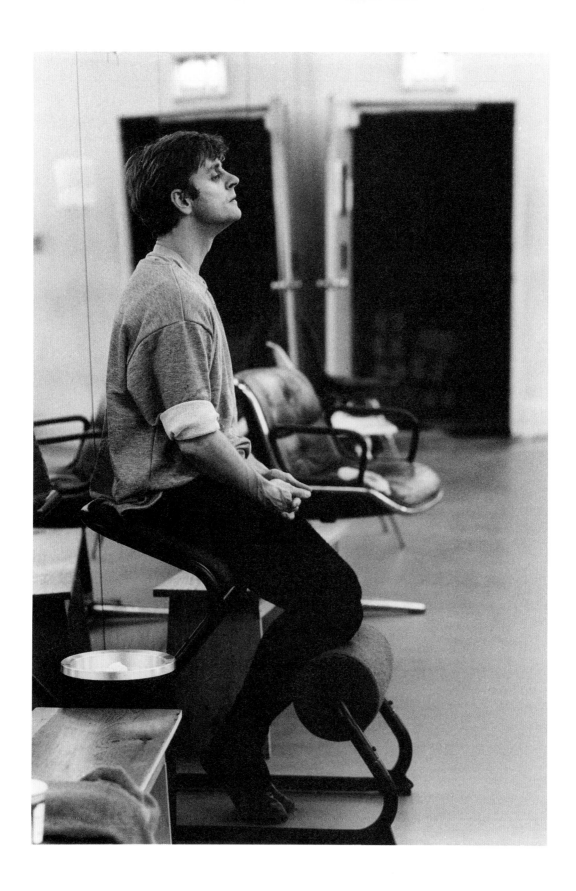

BARYSHNIKOV

PROLOGUE

On June 29, 1974, Mikhail Baryshnikov was dancing with a visiting Soviet ballet troupe in Canada, at the end of a week of performances at Toronto's O'Keefe Centre. Shortly after 11:00 P.M., instead of boarding a bus to go to a postperformance party with his Soviet colleagues, he bolted through a crowd of well-wishers and headed for an automobile, parked near the theater, in which he was whisked away from his Soviet past and into a world of great expectations and beckoning horizons. *Defection* seems such a corrosive and negative word for what was, in effect, the most positive act of the young dancer's life, an act that was joyously received in the West. Yet defection it was, and for several days—as he hid out at a country estate in the middle of an Ontario forest—his fate became the focus of front-page news across the world.

The defection was a remarkable moment for many reasons, including the auguries it held for the future of ballet in North America. It also contained the seeds of this book, although at the time neither the lonely, determined dancer nor this utterly amazed journalist realized it. Our meeting took place right at the beginning—or, at least, the beginning of his third life, the life that started in the West after his Leningrad years, which was the only life he would talk about for a very long time. About his youth in Riga, Latvia—the first life—he kept mostly quiet. Even now he struggles to come to terms with it.

Back in the early summer of 1974, the defection was widely hailed for bringing to the West someone who had already been touted as "the greatest Soviet male dancer since Rudolf Nureyev." Exceptional male dancers are so few in number at any given time that their arrival by whatever means is a major event, one that tends to define their own eras in ballet lore, while their fame quickly spreads well beyond the confines of the expanding but still specialized ballet audience. Baryshnikov's defection constituted a brave personal decision and an authentic historical moment, so it would be appropriate if it could be reported that there was a due sense of solemnity about it all. Appropriate, but inaccurate. There were too many people laughing, one too many crying, a dance critic almost out of control, and an overall scenario more appropriate for *Saturday Night Live* than anything else.

I was then a young dance critic working for the Toronto *Globe and Mail*. Like many other dance writers in North America, I had heard rumors about a Soviet *wunderkind* named Baryshnikov, who had had the same teacher as Nureyev. When it was announced that a provincial ballet troupe from the Soviet Union would be touring Canada and Central America, there was little reason for interest until it emerged that the company would be headed by two stars of Leningrad's Kirov Ballet: Irina Kolpakova and one "M. N. Barichnikoff."

The first performance on the cross-Canada tour was in Ottawa, and I made plans to go to the national capital to see the opening performance and to talk to Baryshnikov. An interview was denied, as it was pointed out that the "correct and polite" procedure was to request a meeting with the touring artistic director, Alexander Lapauri. When the correct request was made, it was quickly granted.

Lapauri was considered an outstanding character dancer in his day. He and his wife, Raissa Struchkova, were particularly well known for their joint appearances in two of the most overwrought of all Soviet choreographic works: *Walpurgis Night* and *Spring Waters*. Struchkova was still being billed in the Soviet Union as a performing prima ballerina at the age of forty-eight, and to no one's evident surprise, she was along on this trip as a star attraction. She also came along for my interview with Lapauri, which got off to a very bad start when I asked if what everyone said about their "boy wonder" was true.

"Who are you talking about?" asked Lapauri, showing seemingly genuine perplexity. "We have many of what you call 'boy wonders' in the Soviet Union." Then, with a manly and self-effacing chuckle, he added, "Why, I myself was once called by such a title!"

He laughed again and looked at his wife, who smiled through clenched teeth that showed the glint of several stainless-steel caps.

"I mean Baryshnikov," I said.

"That one!" said Struchkova, and the great lady turned her head away from me in unfeigned disgust. Lapauri rushed in to get the conversation back on track.

"Mikhail Baryshnikov is, of course, a very exciting young dancer in our troupe, but he is only one of many. . . ."

Here Lapauri wandered off into a string of names and, enjoying the commanding lead he had taken in recapturing the interview, went on to discuss Soviet teaching methods and the perniciousness of the Western star system. As the interpreter droned on in a low monotone, I found myself fixated with the vision of Raissa Struchkova. Was she really going to perform? Would she actually dance with Baryshnikov as her partner? Such things surely weren't possible. It wasn't so much that her considerable age—for a ballerina—was against her. Margot Fonteyn and Alicia Alonso both managed to ride out their illustrious careers for decades on the strength of their well-preserved beauty, great fame, and the seemingly effortless distillation of their years of experience. With Struchkova it was somewhat different. Struchkova had been a beloved ballerina in her prime, and the memory of that prime in the Soviet Union—combined with Lapauri's and her own evident political clout—had been sufficient to mount this strange North American tour, which skirted the United States entirely. But the memory of Struchkova's earlier days was not enough for the mostly young audiences in Canada, who tended to see only her current brawn and unrepentant bravado.

This was no ghostly sylph we beheld. Heaven and her husband alone knew what she tipped the scales at. The sight of her later that evening in full battle dress—spiked tutu, fingers like stilettos set menacingly at the end of her pudding-dough arms and hands, garish smile pasted on her face, her legs surely fashioned from the sturdiest heart of oak—was more than enough to make the strongest men tremble. Literally.

Struchkova's set piece on this tour was the lurid *Walpurgis Night*, the sort of choreography that convinces you finally that there is little point in trying to resist the Soviet menace. The high point in this meat grinder of a *divertissement* comes toward the end, when the leading ballerina flings herself into the waiting outstretched arms of no less than three male dancers. Interpreted by Struchkova, *Walpurgis Night* is not so much a ballet about bacchanalia as it is a reenactment of the siege at Stalingrad. As she prepared to hurl herself into the air at the end, her feet pawed the stage floor. The knees of the three sacrificial males whose job was to safely catch the artistic director's cumbersome spouse were actually shaking. When she finally landed in their arms, the force of the full impact sent them reeling back several steps, and they looked like some potted version of the cygnets in *Swan Lake* trying to carry a steel girder.

Hardly had the full effect of this extraordinary scene sunk in when the curtain at the National Arts Center in Ottawa opened up to reveal Baryshnikov. In Ottawa the audience was not so aware of his reputation as they would be in Toronto and Montreal, where a palpable hush of expectation accompanied the first sight of him. Hundreds of ballet fans in New York were to come to the Montreal performances just to see him, and, as it was learned later, these included at least half a dozen with a special interest in getting beyond the KGB minders who were along on the tour to prevent what ultimately happened.

It was not necessary to know the intricacies of ballet technique to appreciate his brilliance, but those who had studied ballet were nevertheless left staggered at the feats he pulled off. In the pas de deux from *Don Quixote,* which he had to dance with Raissa Struchkova as the youthful Kitri, his solo variations—in which he appeared to be taking a walk in space, using his own technical innovations—caused one of those rare occasions when an audience momentarily did not know how to respond, mere applause seeming somehow inappropriate.

It was following the first night's performance at Toronto's O'Keefe Centre that I walked clumsily into Mikhail Baryshnikov's life. I wish this brief tale, which is not without elements of tension and intrigue, were less of a farce, but it isn't. It also set the mood for our subsequent friendship.

Following the performance at O'Keefe, I returned to my newspaper offices a few blocks away to write up a review of the evening. It was going to be an easy piece to write: Baryshnikov was brilliant, and this had to be celebrated; the Lapauri troupe, on the other hand, was dreadful, and the whys and wherefores had to be itemized. As I sat down at my typewriter, I noticed the message someone had left in the roller: ''Mrs. Barnes from New York says it is extremely URGENT that you call her immediately.''

With a deadline less than an hour away, I was inclined to put the call off until afterward, but curiosity got the better of me. Besides, Mrs. Barnes was Mrs. Trish Barnes, the wife (now divorced) of then *New York Times* dance critic Clive Barnes, and an influential figure in the ballet world in her own right.

''Do you speak Russian?'' she asked after I dialed the New York number.

"*Nyet,*" I replied definitively.

"Well, maybe he speaks some French."

"Maybe who speaks French?"

"Baryshnikov," she said. "You have to get a message through to him tonight or tomorrow. It's absolutely crucial. I tried to do it in Montreal, but the situation was impossible. Use your ingenuity and see what you can do. Have you got a pencil to take down a phone number in New York?"

I got a pencil.

"Tell him his friends want to speak to him," she continued, her voice getting more authoritative as she realized she had me hooked.

"What's up?" I asked. "Is he going to defect?"

"Now look. Don't ask questions. Just get to him. There's no thought of defection. He has three very close friends here who simply have to make contact with him. Remember these names: *Dina, Tina, and Sasha.* Have you got them? *Dina, Tina, and Sasha.*"

"Who are they?"

"Just remember the names. And the phone number. And do be very careful. There may be some nasty people around him."

Right. Now, just *try* to write a review in thirty minutes after a conversation like that.

Somehow words formed themselves as an overactive imagination worked in another sphere altogether, transforming a humble arts writer into the James Bond of ballet. When I reread my review before handing it to the night editor, it was clear to me that I was going to have to strike immediately. The next day would be too late: After this piece was read by Struchkova and her laugh-a-minute husband, there would be no further chance of contact with anyone attached to this company. I think I even managed to say that the state of the corps de ballet represented a setback for Soviet-Canadian relations.

My best chance to nab Baryshnikov, however briefly, was at a reception for the Soviet troupe being given by Seagram's Distilleries in the downstairs foyer back at O'Keefe Centre, and it was there that I sped, faster even than Nureyev fleeing a female admirer. Careful preparations had all been made and I was full of Mountie-like resolve to get my man. To this end, I had written the New York phone number, complete with area code, on one side of a small sticky label. This was carefully anchored to the underside of a signet ring on my right hand. The intention was to shake hands with Baryshnikov at the appropriate moment—*after* turning the sticky side face outward. In this way the paper would stick to his palm as we unclasped. Where this utterly bizarre and foolish idea sprang from, I cannot say. Certainly, it was among the stupidest things I have ever done and came close to being the ruination of the whole exercise.

The reception was going full blast when I arrived—or at least as full blast as a party can go when it is comprised of people who don't understand one another's language. There were about two dozen large round tables set up, with the biggest reserved in the center for the Seagram hosts and their special guests. These included Celia Franca, founder and then artistic director of the National Ballet of Canada, Lapauri and Struchkova, several translators who were considered part and parcel of the KGB—and Baryshnikov.

It was my first sight of him close up, and he looked tired, bored, and frustrated. You can catch exactly the same look on his face today if you pay hundreds of dollars to attend a gala performance of American Ballet Theatre and benefit party afterward. Look for an equivalent central table, the smiling and self-important visage of whoever happens to be chairman of the event, the gleaming countenances of the chief fund-raisers stroking the egos of their selected fund-givers, and then focus on the tired, bored, frustrated Russian expatriate beside them. On most occasions he tries hard to do what is expected of him at these events. Sometimes he doesn't fool anyone. It is at moments like these that I wonder if his life has changed all that much: If you spin on a stage fast enough, high commissars look remarkably like rich capitalists.

A presiding demon deep within me, which was in control of all my minor motor functions that evening, directed me to greet Miss Franca as effusively as possible, so that Baryshnikov would see that I was not some local dupe of his own security agents. If this seems silly in retrospect, it is nevertheless worthwhile pointing out that *glasnost* was not to rear its friendly face for more than a decade. Franca and I had an understanding. I suppose we liked each other well enough, but since I wrote about her company more often than anyone else in the country, I had to allow her periods in which she could dismiss me as an ignorant lunatic of surpassing irrelevance. For her part, she had to put up with my occasional comments about her "vulgar stylistic excesses" and "dictatorial spite." Other than these sorts of things, we had a wonderfully warm relationship during those years.

She was, of course, surprised to see me at the reception, for I never went to such affairs. To this day, I am sure she knew I was up to something.

"You must meet Misha," said Franca, pointing in Baryshnikov's direction. Even at that early date, people felt they had an automatic and immediate right to call him by the affectionate diminutive of his Christian name, Mikhail. At first this practice irritated him, since only his closest friends in Russia would have presumed to use it. In time, however, he got so fed up hearing his proper name pronounced either like a Nazi greeting to a Rolling Stone (Mick-Heil) or like some lost Hebrew prophet (Mick-high-el), that he began encouraging the active use of "Misha."

I had not planned on meeting the quarry quite so soon. Everyone at his table was watching us very closely, and there was no chance of passing anything whatsoever to him. I mumbled a desperate *"bonsoir"* and got one in return, just as a Seagram's official came up to escort me to my assigned spot—far, far away at the edge of the room. It would take me more than half an hour to figure out what to do. On one side of Baryshnikov sat Lapauri, and on the other a very unfriendly-looking translator-*cum*-KGB-minder. Eventually I managed to convince Lapauri that the translator was needed at my table, where a Canadian senator was having problems communicating with the Soviet conductor. When Lapauri himself soon afterward started table-hopping, I saw my best chance. I went straight to where Baryshnikov was sitting and put my hand on his shoulder. He looked at me quizzically as I started saying something in English, until I remembered I was supposed to speak French. Here was the first breakthrough. His French was worse than mine, and we understood each other perfectly. I said the magic three words—Dina, Tina, and Sasha—and his face lit up with the most wonderful amazed smile.

"Ici? Maintenant?" he asked.

"Non, non. À New York. J'ai ici le numéro du téléphone."

I coyly turned the palm of my hand to show him my clever plan. To my horror, the little strip of sticky paper had curled up into a tight ball and was now hopelessly attached to the ring. Trying to look as if I were picking at a wart, I eventually detached and uncurled the damn thing but realized the telephone number was now indistinct. Although I could just make out the figures, I was sure he wouldn't be able to. Baryshnikov laughed out loud. I have heard that laugh many times since and all over the world—in Beijing's Tien An Men Square beneath Stalin's dreadful memorial portrait, in southern Italy and northern Ontario, and all over the United States—but that first time it burst out with such spontaneity that I found myself laughing out loud as well, despite my nervousness. He reached into his jacket pocket and pulled out a notebook.

"Avez-vous un stylo?" he asked me, preparing to write down the telephone number.

Hmmm.

"Non."

A journalist without a pen or pencil, at the center of a great story, must expect to carry a certain amount of emblematic baggage. This was clearly a poorly planned escapade. I turned to the closest table and eventually cadged a stub of a pencil from someone. As Baryshnikov took down the last digits of the telephone number, Franca and Lapauri started walking toward us. Lapauri said something in Russian to Baryshnikov which made the dancer snort cynically and blurt out what I took to be swear words. Later I learned the Soviet artistic director had mockingly asked him: "How much has Celia Franca offered you to join her company?" To which he had replied, "Half a million dollars, but I am holding out for more."

This was all on a Monday evening in June. Four days later, having been contacted by the enigmatic Dina, Tina, and Sasha, he made his historic decision to defect. Even then, the mechanics of defection were not without elements of farce. Sasha, it turned out, was Alexander Minz, a former character dancer at the Kirov and a Jew who had been allowed to emigrate to Israel several years previously and was now part of the New York dance scene. Dina was Dina Makarova, a young woman who always seemed to be doing triple duty as a photographer, a translator, and a personal assistant. She had close ties to American Ballet Theatre and, especially, to the Russian ballerina Natalia Makarova (though they are unrelated), who had defected a few years earlier. Tina was Christina Berlin, the American "love interest," who was also the daughter of a senior Hearst Corporation executive. They had first met in London when Baryshnikov made his Western debut, and she had managed to keep up some sort of relationship with him during the ensuing four years. Together, these three and a small, hastily arranged network of other friends and acquaintances helped create a defection plan, once Baryshnikov had finished his internal struggle and made his decision. The date was to be

Friday, June 29, and the defection would occur as soon as he could get dressed following the final performance at O'Keefe Centre.

As a plan it was simplicity itself—like all great plans that get screwed up. Dina Makarova and a good friend of mine in Toronto named Tim Stewart (whose involvement, like my own, was entirely coincidental) would be waiting in a car parked in front of a nearby restaurant. After the final curtain came down at 10:30 P.M. and Baryshnikov had changed, he would simply walk away from the company. The first leg of the journey would be a speedy drive to a Toronto safe house, where there would be a change of cars, and then the entire entourage would simply disappear into the neighboring country landscape to plan the immediate future in peace and quiet. At his leisure, Baryshnikov could consider his options, deal with the Canadian immigration and security authorities, talk to the artistic directors of ballet companies, and have a brief respite as he started the task of acclimating to his strange new world.

The plan started to go wrong when the stagehands couldn't get the O'Keefe Centre stage curtain open Friday night, delaying the entire performance by fifteen minutes. Then Baryshnikov complicated affairs by dancing too well, garnering curtain calls that stretched out the evening. By the time he got back to the dressing room at performance's end, he was already half an hour late. The couple waiting for him in the car were starting to get agitated and very concerned. One of the KGB minders informed Baryshnikov that he was expected to board a bus as soon as he was dressed, because the entire company was being taken to a civic reception.

In the end, Mikhail Baryshnikov's fans saved the day. A clutch of well-wishers and autograph seekers had blocked a clear passage to the waiting bus, and the dancer was able to use them as a foil to make his escape. While he was running through the adjacent parking lot toward the waiting car, he heard one of the minders shouting out, "Misha! Misha! Where are you going?"

We have been friends ever since. I did the first interview with him following the defection—a difficult but ultimately rewarding assignment in which intense professional pressure to find as melodramatic a story as possible came up against the always tedious restrictions of reality. An editor at my newspaper, for example, was so transfixed by the imagined beauty of the love affair between Christina Berlin and Mikhail Baryshnikov

BARYSHNIKOV AT DAILY CLASS

that protracted negotiations were required simply to explain that the romance was over.

If now, in the rest of this book, I have removed myself almost entirely from the text, it is not because I have grown cold and clinical in my attitude to either Baryshnikov or his company. It is because it is appropriate and less irritating to the reader. The demands of respect and friendship are complicated. Mikhail Baryshnikov gave me enormous trust and assistance during the course of the preparation of this book. In some ways I have repaid him with what might be considered too much scrutiny and analysis. Yet it has been scrutiny built upon a foundation of affection, and there is no point in denying it. This is not a book about ballet, exactly. It is about a group of people who dance for a living. Exotic as their lives may seem, they are our kin. That is how I have always seen them, and that is how I have chosen to write about them.

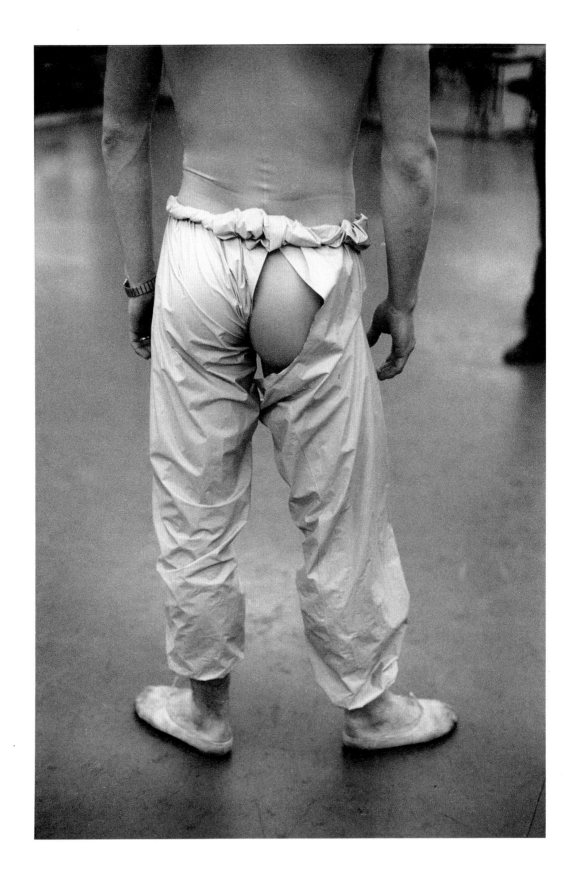

A DANCER WAITING TO REHEARSE

BLAME IT ON BARI

*I*t was not the place you would expect to meet him or them, but there they all were anyway. In Bari, on the detested heel of Italy. During the autumn of 1986, Mikhail Baryshnikov and a carefully selected group of his dancers from American Ballet Theatre entered the heart of ancient Apulia on the Adriatic coast to film a "treatment" of *Giselle* in which the famous ballet would be reworked into a modern, studiously down-market fable of passion aroused and love betrayed. It was a clever idea, everyone agreed, and would give new life alike to a venerable warhorse of the stage and these endlessly topical and marketable dramatic themes.

That, at least, was the theory. There were a lot of theories that autumn in Bari, and one or two of them actually worked out as planned. The movie itself, for example, did get made. Since the veteran film director Herbert Ross was in charge, no one—not the producers, not Baryshnikov, not the dancers, and certainly not the legendary and long-retired dancer Nora Kaye, who was Ross's wife, closest confidante, and the driving force behind the film—was in any doubt that it would get made. On time. Under budget. In the can. Out on general release with an unrestricted rating. Herbert Ross had that kind of reputation. His films usually did nicely, rarely brilliantly. In an age of capricious directors, however, brilliance was often a dubious asset. Herbert Ross was that reassuringly reliable entity: the predictable and safe investment in a financially bizarre and sometimes downright silly industry.

It was the lesser theories, or at least the less expensive ones, that suffered the slings and arrows of outrageous fortune in Bari: the dancers' dreams of a romantic summer in southern Italy; the excitement of a film set; the chance—and you never know—of moving precipitously and triumphantly from the nethermost reaches of the lowly corps de ballet into stardom. Some, if not all, of these hopes inhabited the minds of the beautiful bodies attached to the names appearing on the Bari cast list which had gone up on the company's notice board back in New York, earlier in the year. They should have known better, but who ever does? Especially in a ballet company, even the best one in America. If it were not for dreams, there would not be such a thing as ballet—the cruelest of the performing arts—and mothers would smash their daughters' kneecaps before they had managed even a modest demi-plié.

Florence Pettan knew better, of course, but then she usually did, and besides, she wasn't a dancer. She was a jogger. She also happened to be a member of the artistic director's senior staff at American Ballet Theatre, and she knew from experience how and when to keep her mouth shut, to let the dreams collide with reality at their duly appointed hour. After that cast list appeared, she had her work cut out simply soothing the bruised egos of all those dancers not chosen, and in this bleak category there were many—indeed, the majority of the company. The rejected ones ("Not rejected," the voices from the front office kept saying, in vain. "Simply not selected. . . . It is just a cast list like any other.") succumbed to the usual emotions attendant on such scenes: outrage, paranoia, frustration, jealousy, hurt, unbridled petulance, and a profound sense of unfairness. For many of them, the summer and early autumn would bring the mostly thankless task of scrounging around for part-time work until the company reassembled in the fall, after the filming. This year the task would be made doubly unpleasant by the corrosive realization that others were basking in approbation and potential stardom under the bright Apulian sun.

Although her job is formally spelled out in the ABT prospectus as "Coordinator for Artistic Staff," no one—save the artistic staff itself—thinks of Pettan in that role. Instead, she is the only consistently reasonable and tolerant and loving presence amongst those crucial and demanding senior staff members whose major motivations (from the perspective of the rejected ones) seem only to include holding back careers, avoiding obvious talent, and flagrantly pushing unworthy, unready favorites. When Florence Pettan tells you that the posting of the Bari cast list caused more dissension and bad feeling than any other single event in her experience with the company, it means something. You take notice of anything this woman says that begins "In my experience here . . ." because the experience goes back to when time began. Or at least that is what she says when you quiz her about her enigmatic origins, shrouded as they are in the mists of time and her own artful, utterly endearing obfuscation. In fact, Pettan started at ABT, or Ballet Theatre as it was then called, in the 1950s, when Lucia Chase still ruled supreme—which, given the historical consciousness of most members of the company these days, might as well have been during the Neopaleozoic age.

Later, back in New York after the filming was completed and when everyone on both sides of the issue was a little wiser, dancer Ty Granaroli—who wasn't chosen but couldn't have gone anyway because of an injury and therefore felt free to act as a spokesman—tried to sum up the feelings of the rejected ones by evoking the peculiar notion (peculiar in the hierarchical and dictatorial ballet world anyway) of fairness.

"It wasn't jealousy really," he said. "It was the absurd lack of relationship between the reward of film work and the amount of work put in during the previous season.... You have to realize that in any ballet company, and ABT is certainly no exception, there are dancers who work their guts out during a long and increasingly difficult season, and there are those who coast through—either because they bask in the favor of the artistic staff or, in a very few exceptional cases, because they are so talented they can get away with it. When our people started seeing that the whole long grind simply led to rejection for the single most exciting thing to happen that year, they literally exploded."

"Very bad," said Florence Pettan, nodding gravely when queried about the almighty brouhaha. "No one properly explained that casting a movie is different from casting a ballet, that other considerations come into play. *Giselle* is the smallest of our classical ballets and there were no second or third casts being sent—only one dancer for each role. No one explained that there were budget restrictions. In fact, not many explanations were provided at all, and I would like to think a few lessons were learned as a result."

She paused for a moment and then drew her hand through long auburn hair—or perhaps it was almost titian, for her hair seems to change hue according to the light. It came close to forming a stage curtain across her face and sometimes she just left it there, leaving people in doubt about her expression and mood. This time, though, a clucking Pettan chuckle was emitted as the hair declined to stay in place, a chuckle that seemed to incorporate all at once her innate wisdom, her sense of fate, and benign tolerance for the vagaries of human nature. Florence Pettan is a complex lady. A figure of sheer calm in an artistic office that can sometimes become a bedlam, she is nevertheless ferocious in her defense of dancers. In her eyes none of them can do any real wrong, and she agonizes over their frustrations and depressions just as she rejoices in their triumphs. There is a sweet and innocent theatricality to her presence that seems to endear her to ABT's tyrants and rebels alike. Still a bit vain about her beautiful legs, she is also not above an unabashed display of exotic costume jewelry that on most people might seem excessive, but on her serves as wholly appropriate exclamation marks.

"We're not very good at learning lessons here, you know," she said. "At least not those kinds of lessons. The whole thing could happen again in exactly the same way."

She paused to part the stage curtain again.

"Probably will."

"It's fantastic, don't you think?"

Baryshnikov was excited as his arm swept around the scene before him and took in all of the opulent interior of the turn-of-the-century Teatro Petruzzelli close to the harbor of Bari. Outside, the fading salmon-rouge of this exquisite and still privately owned opera house suggested the onset of genial dilapidation. Inside, however, it had been well maintained, and the requisite gobs of gold and red and marble gleamed under the soft house lights. Statues of local artistic worthies from the last century—their identities now forgotten even by the local staff—adorned the large, ornate entrance. The opera house, which could seat about 1,200 people, seemed much older than its construction in 1891 would suggest. Perhaps it was the charming ersatz cherubim—all flecked with gold right down to their tiniest toes—adorning the tiered balcony light sconces which suggested agelessness. The cherubim, and even the occasional pair of lordly sera-phim at main portals in the orchestra section, surveyed the encroaching and unfamiliar scene below with their accustomed stoic silence. A mostly Italian film and stage crew and a separate group of stagehands were making a great show of industrious activity during a scene change, as if sheer physical endeavor could somehow speed up a process—filming—that was laboriously and notoriously slow. Even on a Herbert Ross shoot, where everything more or less runs on schedule, or else.

"We had such a hard time finding an opera house we could have to ourselves for two months," continued the man often called "the greatest dancer in the world today," who also happened to be the artistic director of the company performing in the film, its lead male dancer, and the star of the sweetly shlocky movie that would later be released as *Dancers*.

Baryshnikov, when he is in his enthusiastic mode, is a deeply engaging and sympathetic figure to be around. When he is relaxed or excited among friends and colleagues, the mantle of his great stardom is worn very lightly. The enthusiasm is infectious and wholly ingenuous, rolling back at least two decades, and possibly three, from his thirty-eight years.

What is not discussed, at least not at this point, is the full nature of the investment Baryshnikov has made in this film. There is a lot at stake for him in it, the least of which is money. There is first of all the matter of a new production of *Giselle* for his company. When the filming is finished, all the sets and costumes will be packed up and sent to New York, where they will be taken over by the company and appear in theaters across America—for up to a decade or even longer, if they prove popular with audiences. On the other hand, the star himself hopes to be making the reverse transition, from stage to screen—he was hinting darkly that he would not be dancing much longer—and this new film, like his two previous efforts, is directly hitched to his mystique and reputation as a ballet star. Essentially, Baryshnikov has played variations of himself, and through this sensible if occasionally mischievous device (for he is not shy in taking advantage of his own notoriety), he has garnered a fair portion of his mass audience. But neither of these films— and *Dancers* would be no exception—had established him as a real film star. A fascinating film presence he was, without any doubt, but the verdict is still out on his acting and awaits a vehicle that is not directly related to his ballet stage persona.

Yet, in the midst of the set in Bari, he seemed blissfully at home. He clearly loves the ambience of film-making, even the small and often tedious details that irritate outsiders—a decision over a camera angle or a somewhat overheated debate on a secondary prop. He works very hard when he is making a film and likes to be seen and accepted by everyone on a shoot—director or grip—as a complete professional. In Bari, it was quickly apparent that there was a dichotomy between the way the film people were able to deal with him and the pattern of contact he has developed with his dancers. The film crowd approached him either deferentially or as equals, depending on their pigeonhole in the temporary hierarchy. The dancers, on the other hand, had to work with a permanent pecking order. When they had specific problems they would come to him directly, *if* he seemed free for a moment—much more directly than they would in America. Otherwise they kept their distance. This is the way

CLASS WITH CANINE FRIEND

DANA STACKPOLE AND ROCKER VERASTIQUE

ISABELLA PADOVANI

CARLA STALLINGS

BONNIE MOORE AND MELISSA ALLEN

SHAWN BLACK AND JOHN GARDNER

Baryshnikov seems to like it, or at least that was the case in Bari. He guards against close-ups in life unless he is with people he absolutely trusts.

"Herbert [Ross] is terrific with the kids, you know," he continued in his exuberant vein. "He is patient. He understands dancers and how to film dancers. He was a dancer himself, and they all feel it. They know he is a choreographer. They have seen his films and they know he's married to Nora. The atmosphere is very good."

And so it seemed, at first sight at least. Up on the stage and back in the wings, however, a young dancer from the corps sat squat on the floor, a shawl around her shoulders to ward off any stray drafts and her silvery-white tutu frumped up to her waist like hydrangea foliage. Her attention was not on the set nor on the director, but on the Russian-born superstar, at least indirectly. This forlorn Wili-in-waiting was reading a book wrapped in a crumpled plain brown paper cover she had obviously fashioned herself in a hurry.

"Looks engrossing. What is it?" said someone on the stage standing behind her.

So engrossing was it that the young dancer was visibly startled and shook from surprise. Then, just like a Chinese dissident caught reading *Time* magazine in a public park, she looked cautiously over her left shoulder and her right shoulder, snapped the book shut, and whispered, "It's Gelsey. I can't put it down."

Gelsey!

Gelsey Kirkland. The greatest partner—after Natalia Makarova—that Baryshnikov had had since his 1974 defection. The woman personally chosen to dance with him "into history" and into the hearts of thousands of ballet fans across America. A beautiful, original, and remorselessly self-driven dancer, she eventually revealed herself as the quintessential "bad girl" of ballet whose unyielding ambition to reach the top had led to a self-destructive relationship with the great men of her profession. A drug dependency and a kind of nightmare existence in which she stumbled alternately between huge success and personal disaster nearly destroyed her career. Hoping to please the luminous choreographer George Balanchine of the New York City Ballet, who had very high standards in ballerinas, she misguidedly had her body altered surgically; for dancer Peter Martins, Balanchine's successor (with Jerome Robbins) at NYCB, who had strange notions of egalitarianism among his lovers, she crouched in shame under bedcovers as he debated her merits with a castoff predecessor; and for Baryshnikov, her second-best ticket to the top (only her own flagrantly abused talent preceded), she succumbed to girlish fantasies, which all came crashing down around her. Toward all of these men with whom she had once been so neurotically insecure, she came to harbor malignant, vengeful feelings, never once pausing to consider herself—the only common denominator in the relationships—as the possible source of her own woes.

In any other country at any other time, Kirkland's travails would have been merely a personal tragedy and the season's grist for the gossip mill. In America during the late summer of 1986, however, they became the stuff of a best seller. Now shrouded in brown paper only a few yards from Baryshnikov himself, a copy of the book—entitled *Dancing on My Grave: An Autobiography*—was being read by a young dancer who could only marvel at being brought so completely into the bedroom of her boss.

''Just take a look at this,'' the dancer said without a trace of coyness. Her sense of awe at the thoroughness of Kirkland's revelations was unsullied by any consideration of ethics or good taste. Still in the midst of the book, it was far too soon for her to ponder whether the writing of it had been a good or proper thing to do. She passed over the torrid offering, opened to the spot where she had been interrupted, her right-hand index finger having served as a temporary bookmark. It was page 127. The notorious page 127, in which the superstar is unbuttoned, unbelted, and unzipped before our very eyes. ''There! That part,'' the young dancer said. ''You can't really believe you're reading it.''

> He seemed embarrassed, like a bashful god [wrote Miss Kirkland of her first sexual encounter with Baryshnikov]. I shared his discomfort and dimmed the lights to conceal my own naked form. Our embrace did nothing to relieve the pressure. This would be our first performance. We were both suffering from stage fright.
>
> I retreated back into the refuge of fantasy, allowing my imagination to guide me through the seduction. We were two statues that had somehow come to life only to dance this intimate pas de deux. The choreography called for us to topple in slow motion onto the mattress. After sliding gracefully beneath the sheets and into each other, the next moment found us hopelessly entangled—like something out of one of those ab-

stract ballets. There was an awkward frenzy of limbs, a struggle for balance and possession. I felt that I had to surrender at this point to his need for control, to his fantasy. . . .

"Stagehands! Clear the stage. *Now!"* Herbert Ross's voice boomed over the public address system from the amphitheater. He asked his young Italian assistant, Michela Nonis, to repeat the order in the local argot. The director was still to learn that the vehemence of his commands was diluted when no one understood what he was saying. In time, when Ross was irritated and wanted speedy action, he would speak to this agreeable and endlessly obliging assistant in a low, menacing growl in order to impress upon her that he was on the edge of an explosion. In one of her endless little acts of cross-cultural diplomacy, the assistant would translate the menace into Italian so baroque in its civility that a Vatican prelate could have used her to tell an erring theologian he was bordering on heresy.

"Director Ross has a request," Michela Nonis would say with a look of apologetic pleading. "He respectfully asks that the stagehands go to the side of the stage with great urgency. He insists upon this point."

Off they went, and for the eighth time that morning, the crew filmed the scene in which Albrecht, the high-born aristocrat who has frivolously enticed the affections of the peasant girl Giselle and led her on a merry dance toward death and the purgatory of the Wilis, approaches her grave site in the middle of an enchanted forest. For the eighth time Mikhail Baryshnikov walked across the stage, strewing lilies in his own path. For the eighth time little clutches of Wilis—spirits representing the romantic sisterhood of spurned lovers everywhere—stood poised in the wings, dressed and coiffed as they had been since 9:00 A.M., waiting for their entrance. For the eighth time the lilies were strewn inadequately for the cameras. For the eighth time Herbert Ross shouted "Cut! Let's do it one more time." He would say it right through to the end of the seventeenth take.

Gelsey Kirkland's book had been carefully placed inside the young dancer's nearby tote bag. She longed to get back to it almost as much as she pined to get onto that damn stage. But it was not to be. Not that day and, thanks to rescheduling, not for another day and a half. And what was it like in romantic southern Italy at the center of a Hollywood film?

"I had no idea how boring it all would be," she said a few days later. "If I'd known, I wouldn't have come. All we do is get dressed up and sit down. We sit around here all day and when I go home at night I feel drained and useless. The only thing we get to see is the inside of this damn theater."

The monologue would go on to form the substance of many post-cards sent home to the rejected ones. To a great extent, such terse but informative messages mollified the jealousy and assuaged the hurt. Florence Pettan knew that the dancers themselves would sort things out, in time. Meanwhile, there was still Kirkland's ghastly but hypnotic book to be perused, and it served its own little purpose in relieving the tedium of the seemingly endless nights in less-than-beautiful Bari.

When it came to the moment that Baryshnikov would actually dance in the film, the threat of anticlimax and even catastrophe stalked the premises, at least initially. The day for Baryshnikov's Act Two extravaganza—in which Albrecht is driven to the brink of death by the Wilis, until he is saved by the redeeming quality of Giselle's love—did not begin well. This is an understatement, for he was in one of his "Russian moods," the sort of spectral sulk that seems to have a physically tangible aura capable of sucking unsuspecting victims into its vortex if they dare to come closer than three yards. People who wanted his attention—a minion from the film director, Baryshnikov's masseur, a costume repairer—hovered outside the danger zone. Under such circumstances, it is widely held to be unwise to posit genial little pleasantries such as "Had a bad night, Misha?" Still, someone said just that and the response was revealing.

"You bastard," he said, with the bantering and crude affection which is the tip-off that part of the mood, some of the time, is for pure effect. "I'm a crippled old man and you want to make fun of me." There followed his usual string of expletives, many fractured beyond recognition in a weirdly triumphant Anglo-Russian syntax that would send a church contralto swooning, but were in fact a talisman of friendship and trust. He was unmasking himself and admitting to the extraordinary pain involved in his endeavors, thanks to the attrition and injuries his body suffered over the years of his greatest fame. It was not a complicated problem he was facing, merely an inexorable one. If you jump higher than anyone else, it follows as tritely as night does the day that you fall harder.

Baryshnikov was a dancer audiences felt could defy gravity. This was the cruelest illusion of all, because gravity and age had stored up for even the greatest dancer of our age a pitiful reckoning.

As he massaged sore muscles on a leg that had been operated on several times and which was, at long last, becoming almost impossible to deploy the way he wanted to, he snapped at himself for arousing even a hint of concern. "Don't look so worried, you son of a bitch. I may not be able to do *Don Quixote* the way I would like to anymore, but I can still do a good *Giselle*. I know the difference. Just watch."

The bravado was as phony as the sulk. Baryshnikov's professionalism is his single purest quality and is underscored by an effortless facility for technical self-evaluation and criticism. He simply would not have agreed to do the film, or dance this day, if he had not thought he would do both well. The consequences were irrelevant; either he could do it, or he couldn't. He brings the same realism to his evaluation of the dancers who work for him and is constantly surprised when one of them resents what for him is obvious and straightforward.

Did he soar less high in Bari than in earlier years, as he traversed the insubstantial firmament and universe that fills the yawning cavity of the stage? Maybe. Yet he gave his all, and Baryshnikov's all at thirty-eight still provided the definition of a vision that holds that the imagination can be transformed through a relentlessly structured combination of art, physical agility, and personal commitment. If, as he would probably say himself, he has danced *Giselle* technically better than he did in Bari, that is not the issue. The point is that throughout the tedious process of filming, in which he had to repeat sequences he had done with seeming flawlessness, there was precisely that same controlled fire and harnessed fury that sent him hurtling around the stage when North American audiences first saw him dance, in Canada, with a Soviet troupe a week before his defection. That was twelve years and a lifetime earlier. To have seen the black mood of the morning deployed on the awesomely haunted face of Albrecht, struggling between reason and guilt, and pleading for redemption, was to have understood the technique and process of stage metamorphosis. To have witnessed the suffering technician swallow his pain and accommodate physical limitations was to have explored the intimate structure of professional and personal courage. Most dramatically, to have stepped back and found oneself swept away by the beauty and pathos of what some might consider an archly romantic fairy tale, simply through the willful determination of one man's unyielding commitment, was to travel into the heart of a hundred mysteries that bind the very substance of art and the human condition.

And this he did during three days in Bari. When it was done, he grinned like a boy who had just scored the winning goal in a junior-league hockey playoff.

"There, you bastard! Not so bad for a crippled old man."

"Misha, you're no help to me up there right now. Would you please . . . Misha? *Misha?* Are you listening to me?"

It was Herbert Ross talking. He was trying to get the stage cleared, and Baryshnikov was still talking to several of his dancers about a technical point in the sequence that had just been filmed. Only the dancers noted the tone of irritated impatience in Ross's voice. Only the dancers noted immediately the significance of the fact that their artistic director had just been talked to as if he were a naughty boy, had been talked to just the way he sometimes talked to them. They said nothing, but it was possible to gauge the tension—and especially the anticipation. It was intense. Baryshnikov stopped talking and just kept looking at the floor.

"Misha?" asked Ross again.

The Russian turned on his heel and faced stage front, exactly where Ross was facing. His face was flushed red with anger and embarrassment. He put his hands on his hips. "Herbert," he said, "don't you dare ever talk to me like that again. Here or anywhere. Do you understand?"

There was a long silence. Only the Italians chattered, but one by one they stopped, too, as partial translations spread around the set. Ross, once again caught out with the confused dancers of American Ballet Theatre somewhere along twin avenues of authority (to him as the movie director, to Baryshnikov as artistic director), was no fool and knew how to cut his losses.

"Misha," he said, "I'm very sorry. Let's get on with our film."

Baryshnikov thought about this for about five seconds, took a breath, and turned around to his dancers. "Yah," he said, "that's a good idea. Let's get on with our film."

Later he told one of his artistic staff that he wasn't actually angry at Ross (untrue), but that he knew he had to make something of a scene for the sake of his position among his dancers (the truth).

*   *   *

She walked in beauty, no doubt about it, for her face and bearing could have come straight from a high Renaissance portrait. A later and happier Capulet virgin, you might think, discovered at the precise moment when her father had snared the finest prince of Verona with an unrivaled dowry. Was she twelve or twenty? That shining, translucent face skittered between girlish shyness and the knowing, enticing impetuosity of someone with suitors to spare. Julie Kent of Potomac, Maryland, was not yet out of her teens, had spent less than a year in the company—in the corps de ballet at that—and had precious little stage experience, yet so elegant and obvious was her beauty that she had been chosen for a lead role opposite Baryshnikov in the film.

Among the rejected ones, and even among some of those who had made it to Bari, she had been catapulted into instant notoriety. "What transpired on the casting couch?" asked some. "It was a scandal," insisted others. "She's just a child." Often enough this "child" sat alone in the opera house amphitheater, warily sensing the whispers circulating above and around her. Someone, somewhere, had astutely instilled sufficient strength of character into Kent to help her withstand both the real and the imagined brickbats. She knew what people were saying, she said, and it didn't really matter because she had been chosen and had not in any way schemed for the role, a role that would in a very short time give her more exposure to more people than even a lifetime on the ballet stage could offer.

There was only one genuinely substantial problem on Julie Kent's promising horizon, and it became painfully evident every time she opened her mouth. God had given her beauty; her parents and teachers had given her self-confidence and commanding poise; Mikhail Baryshnikov and his advisers had given her the role of a lifetime; but no one could do anything about a voice that squeaked and grated like a rusty hinge. There was certainly something that might laughingly be called an intellectual awareness of the problem, but in a Herbert Ross film, deep into production, no consideration was given to recasting the role. Instead, in one of those curious bits of ambivalent logic, it was argued that the voice problem was in fact an asset, adding a special element of reality to a film story not otherwise burdened by much verisimilitude. By the time the rough cuts were completed and it was apparent to all those with ears to hear that The Voice had all the charm of slate-screeching chalk, the rationale of "honest realism" would be stated even more vociferously. It was as if all those believing in the film could somehow will the patently unacceptable to become the possible.

Unfairly, Kent's ordinary speaking voice did not seem unduly inappropriate. If it deflated somewhat the sense of mystery and appeal her eloquent beauty instantly aroused, it nevertheless fitted the genuine reality of a young American dancer of the late eighties who was fresh into the company. People are all of a piece, and taken in the whole, we usually accept them as they are. It was the exclusive focus of the camera and the disembodying microphone that played so much havoc here, but it would require the derision and condescension of film reviewers before the obvious hit home. There was no terrible price for Kent to pay in this business, however. The reviewers also noted her beauty and presence, and her career as a dancer is proceeding apace much as it would have had she never appeared in the film. She was undoubtedly aware, too, of a cautionary and parallel tale half a decade earlier, when Leslie Browne played opposite Baryshnikov in his first film, *The Turning Point*. Browne had been admired, and many predictions were made about the success of her immediate future. In fact, she had a hard time recovering from such massive early exposure, and it would not be until the upcoming season of 1986–1987, back in the United States, that Leslie Browne would finally come into her own.

Still, the squeak that squelched a dozen decibels also served its part in healing the internal bleeding of the rejected ones back home. The balm of pure malice should never be underestimated.

''This isn't really what Ballet Theatre is like,'' said Florence Pettan as one of the young dancers flounced offstage followed by her newfound court of stylish young men picked up, God knows where, on the streets of Bari. Pettan wasn't being defensive, merely descriptive. The dancer's retinue had been preceded by the arrival of Charles K. McWhorter, the president of Ballet Theatre Foundation, Inc., which is responsible for the company's financial operation. One of the most senior officials of American Telephone & Telegraph Company and a prominent elder worthy of the Republican party, McWhorter was evidently in a festive mood. His royal-blue crushed-velvet jump suit perfectly set off a stunning and extensive collection of designer silver jewelry as he explained who was who on the film set to a companion. It was all for theatrical effect, no doubt, for back in New York at the annual ABT board meeting at the Metropolitan

Opera House, McWhorter was the soul of respectability in a sober gray business suit, and his devotion to the company has helped see it through many a bleak financial crisis. It was only because Florence Pettan saw a jaw drop as the passing circus came into view that she hastened to put things into perspective.

"It's Bari," she insisted. "Everyone's more relaxed. We're all business in New York. That's where everyone has a home and a real life. This is sort of a more exotic version of what it's like when we go touring. You'll see. As a company, we have a many-faceted personality!"

She winked and there was only a slight trace of the devil in her eyes. "Oh, thank heavens. There's Charles. I've got all sorts of messages for him from New York. *Charles!* I need to speak to you now."

"What is it, Florence? You can see I'm busy."

The first sight and sound of Charles France, referred to by many of the New York ballet cognoscenti as "the notorious Charles France," is unforgettable, and familiarity makes that first impression no less memorable. In time, though, his sheer Falstaffian bulk recedes from the consciousness as a man of Byzantine complexity and staggering single-mindedness of purpose takes over. France also has his official designation in the company literature. It states that he is "Assistant to the Artistic Director." To give some idea of how understated this job description is, the New York dance critic Clive Barnes can always get a rise from his audience—and the company—when he slyly refers in print to the "Baryshnikov–France artistic directorship."

For some people, including a few dancers and members of the board from inside the company, France represents the dark side of the Baryshnikov legend and the Baryshnikov leadership of ABT. He is referred to as "The House Rasputin" or "Misha's Svengali." This is something that goes far beyond the traditional malice felt toward any second-in-command, who often enough is required to wield the hatchet for his only superior. When people, like a couple of "Friends of American Ballet Theatre" (financial supporters) in Los Angeles, catch sight of France and Baryshnikov together and are told this is the most important person in the superstar's professional life, they react—mostly from the sheer incongruity of the physical contrast—with startled disbelief bordering on horror. And if a "Russian mood" is something to make grown men tremble, to be around when a "France snit" is being deployed makes the former condition seem akin to a pastoral idyll. Yet what has never been known outside the company is the degree to which this extraordinary man has transformed himself—mind, spirit, and body—in the service of his art, his company, and his artistic director. There is about Charles France the aura of a gifted absolutist.

As Florence Pettan was trying to get France's attention that particular afternoon in Bari, he was deep in conversation with Nora Kaye, who, in addition to her wifely duty to keep Herbert Ross sane, was also involved in casting for the film and generally using her keen and experienced eye to spot problems or come up with solutions. Actually, when France said he was busy, he was not being strictly truthful. He was actually telling dirty jokes to Kaye, who was laughing so heartily that tears were coming down her cheeks.

Simultaneously, as Pettan tried to detach France from this unseemly endeavor, Ross was getting angry at the background noise. "Quiet, goddammit!" bellowed the director.

"Please, everybody," said the assistant in Italian. "Director Ross respectfully requests strict silence."

Nora Kaye rolled her eyes in mock terror as she and France broke out into another round of laughter, and the director winced.

Anyone detaching that little scene and holding it up in isolation for scrutiny would have been appalled by the dirty jokes and amazed by the infantilism of these two pivotal figures in the dance world. Only a few observers knew that Kaye, who embodied so much of the glorious hustle and élan of Ballet Theatre's own past, was suffering from cancer that autumn in Bari and would die before the company's New York season was launched, a season that would be dedicated to her memory. Charles France knew, and he adored this woman both for her own sake and also for what she represented in the history of ballet in America. In her final, painful days, when many pressing decisions awaited his attention, Charles France busied himself with the humble task of making Nora Kaye laugh. It was an act of pure love.

Laughter was in fact what kept most people sane in Bari during the filming, but analyzing humor is a deadly business. For Baryshnikov and France and their *ad hoc* entourage, for example, the longest sustained joke was an unexplainable and ferociously filthy sequence of puns built around the French word for lesbian. Anyone and everyone invited into their small circle was drawn remorselessly into this juvenile exercise. It was humor of the moment, wild and outrageous, and clearly created to let off steam from the heightened emotions and frustrations created by the laborious filming.

Somewhat more fruitful, but only just, was the second-longest sustained joke. This was the ridiculous effort to come up with a name for the damn project other than *Giselle* itself. The senior artistic staff, driving down the rugged coast from Bari on a Sunday outing, put their minds to the task. Some of the suggested titles, reeking of sarcasm and the week's little dramas, seemed as sophisticated as a pair of Gucci sock garters. Two of the names from the film script attracted particular attention: Nadine, the film name for the ballerina who dances Myrta, Queen of the Wilis; and Muriel, who dances Giselle's mother. From this insubstantial material came *Ciao, Muriel; Muriel and Nadine in Italy; No, No, Nadine;* and the personal favorite of Charles France, *Myrta, She Wrote.* In honor of producer Jack Brodsky, who had also been behind the enormous hit *Romancing the Stone* and whose single-minded concentration on box-office appeal had been duly noted, Baryshnikov himself came up with *Romancing the Tombstone.*

And, as if this weren't bad enough, other title suggestions sank to the level of *Blame It on Bari, Grand Delusions, Miracle on Cavour Street* (to commemorate the location of the opera house), and, probably worst of all, *Et Tu, Tutu.*

Lisa Weisinger was standing her ground, and so was Charles France. It was a couple of weeks before the troupe in Bari were supposed to return to New York. Weisinger is the company manager, responsible for an endless array of small details, from travel arrangements to counting the box-office receipts at all of the theaters ABT finds itself dancing in throughout the year. Her department hands out the paychecks, determines the rates of overtime costs, and coordinates all the disparate items involved in a move from one city to the next. It also arranges for the special seating and ticket requests that daily afflict such an important company wherever it is performing. If you are an important pooh-bah in Tampa who might conceivably be a donor to ABT, and at the last minute you and your mistress want to see the ballet when the performance has been sold out for weeks, then ultimately it is Lisa Weisinger who has to be toadied up to and who also has to determine which unfortunate folk inside the company will be turned out of their seats.

On this occasion, however, she was engaged in a peripheral but heated verbal brawl with France that had much to do with internal company politics. Many of the dancers, having "worked their butts off" on the *Giselle* filming schedule in Italy, suddenly became concerned that they were only being allowed three hours in Rome before flying back home. Weisinger had jumped in to intercede on their behalf so they could at least have one day and one night in the Eternal City.

"I don't see it, Lisa," said France, who was clearly irritated at this attempted diversion from the company's well-laid plans, designed to accomodate a rigorous rehearsal schedule for Sir Kenneth MacMillan's new production of *The Sleeping Beauty*. He may also have been annoyed at the prospect of yet again being seen in the role of villain by the dancers. For a company manager to be in conflict with the artistic management represented potential trouble, and France brought the full weight of his forceful personality to the ensuing wrangle. "We will have to change all the reservations, pay for the hotel rooms, and probably spend hours trying to track down people who have got lost. We need them on the plane as we planned and back in New York in time to get a few days' rest before rehearsals start."

"I think that's quite unreasonable, Charles, if you don't mind my saying so," said Weisinger. They were talking in the orchestra section of the Teatro Petruzzelli, and France shifted his great bulk in the inadequate seat while simultaneously pushing his glasses back to the top of his nose.

"What do you mean it's unreasonable? This isn't some cultural tour of the historical relics of Italy, you know. Everyone understood from the beginning what the schedule was. I don't understand why you are making difficulties now."

"First of all, they are prepared to pay for the hotel themselves and I don't mind changing the reservations," persisted Weisinger. "I've already checked with the airline and it won't be a problem. So why don't you try and see this from their viewpoint."

"I *am* looking at it from their viewpoint, goddammit. I want them back in New York and ready for rehearsals. It's a very heavy rehearsal schedule and I don't want them arriving back exhausted and disoriented the day before. Have you ever heard of jet lag?"

"Charles, I think you are being very unreasonable about this. . . ."

Finally, he couldn't take any more. He heaved himself up into a standing position, gathered up his papers, and glared at Weisinger, who probably knew from the beginning that this moment was coming.

"I don't want to discuss it anymore. Do it as we originally planned."

"Charles . . ."

"Do it!"

"You mean they can stay in Rome?" asked Weisinger, in a gloriously futile last stab.

Charles France looked up to the ceiling of the Teatro Petruzzelli to see if God, or at least a minor southern Italian deity or saint, would strike this infernal woman deaf and dumb.

"Please change nothing. Leave everything as it is—was. They go home as planned. You go home as planned. I go home as planned. Mikhail Baryshnikov goes home as planned. Nothing is changed. Nothing will be changed. There are good reasons for this, Lisa."

In the end, many of the dancers did manage to fit in a two-day trip to Rome thanks to changes in the film schedule—and did so with management approval. Weisinger would later cite this encounter as a perfect example of the difficulty of dealing with Charles France. For his part, France would talk about it as an example of how to score easy points with the dancers at the expense of what he believed was good for the company as a whole.

Florence Pettan was right. People's chemistry changes when they are far away from home, in a group, and on the prowl. A kind of summer camp atmosphere sets in, factions form in an instant, and the revels of the moment take on a degree of significance that seems embarrassing in retrospect, if they haven't actually been obliterated from the memory. To an outsider, and certainly to many of those participating for whom filming was not a way of life, much of the activity in Bari seemed definitely brain-dead. Yet the participants seemed to learn quickly how to pace themselves, and after a few weeks even carping became ritualistic and harmless.

There was also the question of mental attitude, which for some of the dancers—the ambitious ones anyway—relieved the torpor occasioned by their duties. Few could have had a more tedious task than Wes Chapman, a young dancer from Union Springs, Alabama, who had first joined ABT three years previously. Chapman's job, when he wasn't frolicking as a peasant with his stupid garland, was the essentially humiliating one of holding the spot on the stage where Baryshnikov would normally be while the director set up his shots. Sometimes this required Chapman to lie prone on the floor for the better part of an hour. At other times he had to maintain unnatural positions or balance precariously beside the dreaded revolving grave. But Chapman didn't mind it, or at least that's what he said, and there is no reason to disbelieve him.

"It was an honor, really. Don't laugh! I was thrilled when I was chosen to come to Bari. This isn't the sort of work we normally have a chance to do, and you can learn a lot just listening and watching."

He laughed when he said this as he toted up all the listening and watching he had done so far. Like many, if not most, of the men dancing in American Ballet Theatre, he had been sustained not just by his own determination to have a career in ballet, but by one singular event: He had seen Mikhail Baryshnikov dance. Love him or hate him, and everyone at ABT does both at some time, this singular, elusive, playful, brooding, egotistical, and self-deprecating Russian is the shining sphere around which everyone and everything orbits. It is a role he would gladly shirk, and often tries to. Yet the complicated structure of his commitment to this company and to ballet itself has rarely been explored, except to be doubted. Few people know he works at ABT for nothing—not one red cent. Few people know how he craves to be freed from the prison of daily exercise and the worsening pains in his body. Too many people feel they know nearly every detail of his social and love life, but they did not see him when he made his decision to come West, when he was green and raw in the ways of the world and a favored brat of the Soviet Union's cultural elite. If there had been premeditation leading up to that act, the decision was nevertheless emblematic of the boldness which has been the hallmark of his career. And at the very last moment, he still had to make his legs walk away from the only life he knew. The unknown is not everyone's favorite destination.

BARYSHNIKOV AND TIM-THE-DOG AT CLASS IN WASHINGTON, D.C.

ENIGMA IN A RIDDLE

Mikhail Nikolaievich Baryshnikov was born in Riga, Latvia, on January 27, 1948, the son of a Soviet army officer and a mother Baryshnikov himself describes as "a simple woman." His earliest years are particularly hard to recover because, for all practical purposes, there is only one authority on them and that is the dancer himself. As the prime source, of course, he is invaluable, but also subject to the vagaries of memory. Like anyone else summoning up a remembrance of things long past, Baryshnikov must rely on a memory governed by convenience, nostalgia, anger, and the distorting filter that allows us all to place ourselves at the center of the stage. On the other hand, he is very open about his past, and has trained himself since coming to the West to understand the need for a context, so his childhood memories have a pungency and cogency that fully suffice until a more impartial source emerges—which will probably never happen.

His father, who remarried following the death of his first wife (Baryshnikov's mother), died in 1981, but the dancer had cut most of his ties to him long before he defected in 1974. He has no sense of loss for a particular family, intimately known, and had none even while he was there, so that if he broods morosely on things past from time to time—and he does—it is for kith, not kin. His friends and teachers became his family, and they were a diverse lot, quite a few of whom also came West either before or after he made his own leap. There is irony here. He fled the Soviet Union for freedom, yet like all his countrymen who find themselves in "exile" in the West, he has to be allowed a certain amount of wistfulness for Mother Russia. This is symbolized most tangibly by the effort and money he has lavished on creating a kind of superior Russian *dacha* with his house beside the Hudson River. Even his stylish studio apartment in New York, with its eighteenth-century prints of St. Petersburg, its Russian books, its theater designs and heavy period furniture, lends further substance to the notion of an expatriate pining for a lost home. Not too much should be made of these obvious things, however, because the nature of his attachment to his homeland is only nominally sentimental. Russian *objets* and Russian style are purchasable and offer the comfort of familiarity. Yet in Russia, Mikhail Baryshnikov was a Yankee-phile who pined for an America of the imagination which anyone from the United States could have told him didn't exist, but which—with characteristic obstinacy—he ultimately created for himself.

"I longed for America," he said shortly after his defection, and this was in Canada, before he had yet made it south of the border. His Russian was punctuated by American-English slang, and there was even a quint-essential American movie hero in his life—in a joking aside concerning his defection he described himself as feeling like "Steve MaWheen" in *The Getaway.* "Except," he said, "I didn't get the girl or the money." Steve McQueen would no doubt have been flattered that the admiration went so far as to include Baryshnikov's version of the actor's swagger and facial expressions.

The fascination he had for American popular culture, which a num-ber of observers since the defection have attributed to subsequent events and the spoiling factor of success, was in fact nurtured for years in a society that offered him, as it does most of its greatest artists, everything material that America could provide—relatively speaking—but none of its freedom of spirit. In truth, there has never been a time in Mikhail Baryshnikov's life when he has not been regarded as special. The miracle is not that instances of studious selfishness in his personality can still be cited, but that in most respects he is so normal, accommodating, generous, and such genuinely good fun. Or at least he is most of the time, when people who want or need a part of him aren't pestering him with requests for things he would rather not do. If you can catch him between lovers (the beginnings and endings of his affairs not being the ideal time to discuss international politics or existential philosophy), he is a friend for all seasons—with an arching, exuberant love for the variety and potential of merely being alive that is wholly infectious. If his notoriously bleak Russian moods are special, so are his riotous highs.

Baryshnikov was certainly special at the time of his birth, if for no other reason than that he was born of Russian parents in a country Joseph Stalin occupied during the Second World War. Thus, through fate, he became part of the structure of a hated occupation. Latvia had been a prosperous and reasonably democratic state for most of this century leading up to the war. Unfortunate, like all the Baltic states, in its diminutive size and geographical proximity to the Soviet Union, Latvia had first been forced to make its accommodation with Hitler's Germany. It is a measure of the cruelty visited on the Latvians by the subsequent Soviet invaders, who supplanted the detested fascist regime in Riga at war's end, that given a choice between these two monster dictators, the Latvians would reluctantly have had to choose Hitler.

Although the Soviet occupying forces were ruthless and brutal, Baryshnikov has no real knowledge of his father's direct involvement in the tragedy visited on this tiny country. Probably it was peripheral, given the elder Baryshnikov's duties as a military instructor. The son knows only that this stern and cold figure was an enthusiastic army man and an extreme Soviet nationalist who took all his rights in Riga for granted. He remembers his father as both a voluble anti-Semite and a despiser of Latvian national consciousness. These aversions were a source of deep embarrassment to Baryshnikov, because, as a boy, he had mostly Latvian and Jewish friends. The pattern of making unsuitable friendships and generally doing things that cut across the pattern of prescribed expectations surfaced early and remains with him today. Most Russian children at that time would have had nothing to do with the conquered population. Most boys do not decide by themselves to study ballet. Most Russian dancers do not defect. Most superstars in the West do not elect to forsake the fast road to success to explore different modes of choreography simply for the sake of their art. Most classical dancers eschew popular entertainment as somehow demeaning. At no time in his life has Baryshnikov been content to conform with what was expected of him. He has always embraced that curious, contradictory, and explosive combination of sporadic rebellion and diligent submission to duty which not only creates a great dancer but extends the horizons of what had hitherto been thought possible.

His childhood, he would tell friends, was strange, and the fact that he was a product of the hated conquerors but preferred to make his friends among the conquered encouraged a seemingly natural capacity for play-acting and disguise. Somehow, he seemed able to will himself to be something—and someone—other than what he was. He learned to speak Latvian well and was sufficiently observant, even at a young age, to notice the difference between the stolid and predictably dour way the Soviets in Riga dressed and the more stylish—albeit often homemade—clothes of the Latvians. His disguise included everyday clothing and he took on local coloring. Because his father could be counted on to say embarrassing or rude things to any friend who was not Russian, Baryshnikov also became adept at keeping his friends away from his home—unless he knew his mother was there alone, and then a different universe unfolded.

He adored his mother, and time has only reinforced the meager store of his earliest memories of her. In his eyes she was "beautiful: tall and blond—stunning," as he told Arthur Gold and Robert Fizdale, longtime friends and neighbors of Baryshnikov who interviewed him for *Vanity Fair*. Uneducated, his mother nevertheless loved going to the opera and the ballet, and she usually brought her son with her, despite the fact that he could barely sit still through the opera. Ballet, on the other hand, had an athletic component that appealed to him instantly. Short as he was, he was an enthusiastic soccer player who also managed to join in on team fencing and gymnastics, for which he apparently showed considerable flair. Much of it was "after-class" activity, and when he was around the age of ten—he cannot remember exactly when it was—he stumbled into a folk-dancing group. It would be agreeable to be able to report that this first taste of dance is what led directly to his extraordinary career in ballet, but Baryshnikov says this is not the case. The appeal of folk dancing was two-fold. First, his father liked and understood it, and so it formed one of the very few means the son ever found to arouse paternal pride and approval. Second, folk dancing led directly to girls.

A year or so later, he decided on his own at the age of eleven to try out at a local choreographic school to see what would happen. There was no pressure from his mother, but when his father found out, there was trouble. The elder Baryshnikov was upset, but not for reasons a Western father might be upon discovering that his attractive, athletic son wanted to put on dancers' tights. The elder Baryshnikov wanted his son to follow a career that made sense, took advantage of his position in Soviet society, and was the natural consequence of hard work at school.

The flaw in this plan was that Mikhail Baryshnikov simply didn't do very well at school. Although he liked history and literature, he consistently disappointed his father in mathematics and science. To avoid homework he "cheated and lied," and these perceived character flaws brought far more paternal wrath down upon the son's head than anything else he did, including dancing. In the midst of this period, the major calamity of his life occurred. His mother died. And she didn't just die, hard as that would have been for a doting boy who was still a year away from his teens. She committed suicide. "Actually," as he eventually discovered, "she hanged herself."

Why she did it, he still doesn't really know, but the effect of the deed remains with him and invests many small moments with unexpectedly complicated emotions. At a dinner table in Bari with close friends, the cover picture on a paperback book a friend had brought along sent him spinning reluctantly back to a specific past that was only then becoming more tolerable to remember. He can only speculate on why she took her own life. There was, perhaps, a period of mental instability, and he can remember that she cried easily and often during her final months. But it is the last glimpse he had of her at the railway station in Riga that has become implanted on his consciousness with such riveting clarity. That was what the picture on the book jacket aroused. The book itself was an account of life in Paris under the Nazi occupation, but the black-and-white jacket was built around a 1944 photograph: In the background, uniformed German soldiers are talking to—possibly questioning—an anonymous citizen. In the foreground, a Parisian woman stands on the Pont Alexandre III, looking out over the Seine toward the Left Bank and caught by the camera in profile. She is young, tall, probably blond, and wearing as smart a tailored skirt and jacket as might have been found at the time.

"That's Mother!" exclaimed Baryshnikov, who grabbed the book and pored over the picture, barely able to accept the truth that it wasn't who he thought it was. "That's how I remember her the final day, the last time I ever saw her. We were all supposed to be going away for a holiday, but at the last minute I learned Mother wasn't coming. There seemed to be no reason for this, and Father wasn't the sort of man to answer any questions. Somehow I didn't really understand she wasn't coming until I was actually on the train with Father and turned around to see that Mother was still on the platform. She was crying and the tears were pouring down her face. And I started crying too. I couldn't stop my own tears. I remember it very clearly. Then the train began to move and she walked a little way beside it while it was still going slowly. Finally she just stopped walking, and we became farther and farther apart. She kept waving, and in my mind she was never more beautiful.

"That was it. I never saw her again. By the time I returned from the holiday with Father, she was dead. She killed herself, and I have never really known the reason why. For me at the time, it was the end of my life."

The end of his first life at least, because before a year was out a successful choreographic examination had brought him into contact with the first of two ballet teachers in the Soviet Union who would take control of his second life. The teacher's name was Yuri Kapralis, and for three years in Riga, Kapralis, who was still a dancer, gave Baryshnikov the basics of his technical training. He was clearly something of a hero to the boy and came to be regarded almost as an older brother. Baryshnikov was also heavily influenced by the excellent character teacher Valentin Blinov, whom he adored as a father, and in whose classes he excelled. Ironically, his relations with his actual father subsided into an acceptable compromise during this period. They ate breakfast together with a certain measure of mutual civility and this was—for the most part—the sum total of their daily contact. It was sufficient to keep the peace.

By the time Baryshnikov turned fifteen, it was clear to teacher and pupil that the small provincial school in Latvia was not going to be able to meet either the needs or the demands of the prodigious talent that was emerging. There was only one place considered appropriate and that is where he went. In retrospect, Leningrad was simply inevitable.

At the Leningrad Ballet School, generally considered the foremost ballet academy in the world, Baryshnikov came under the sway of Alexander Pushkin, Rudolf Nureyev's mentor and indeed one of the most illustrious teachers of male dancers in this century. The institution the young Baryshnikov now came to regard as his real home had not only the full weight of high Soviet approbation to recommend it, but also came complete with a history and a tradition going back to 1738, when it was first created to train dancers for the courts of the czars in St. Petersburg. The Leningrad Ballet School is still located at its famous precincts on Theatre (now Rossi) Street, and it was from this singular and sturdy dancers' redoubt that so much of what Westerners associate with the classical ballet first emerged. That extraordinary generation of Russian dancers, first trained by Marius Petipa and later brought to the unsuspecting West by Serge Diaghilev in 1909 for the first Ballets Russes season in Paris, got all its training here, and it is still considered the sine qua non of such establishments.

Pushkin's reputation was at its peak when Mikhail Baryshnikov walked into the school for the first time. No demonstration of the boy's technique was required. It happened that Pushkin had a class for boys his age. There was a conversation and a physical examination, and he was in. From that first day, he said goodbye to his boyhood home in Riga, except for rare visits to his remarried father, and he had no regrets. This, too, established a precedent for him, because if there was any longing for friends or old haunts, it was utterly eradicated in the relentless demands placed upon him in the school. Years later, when he defected, the ferocious energy he deployed in dancing anywhere in anything he could latch onto paralleled these early years at the Leningrad Ballet School. He had found another father figure in Pushkin, who responded with warmth and the sort of challenges Baryshnikov lusted to meet head-on.

"Pushkin was not a terribly complicated man," Baryshnikov would later recall fondly. "Although the mechanics of his teaching method may have appeared mysterious to some, they nevertheless would lead a dancer to the right solution."

"He had a good eye for what's right and what's wrong, but he couldn't explain," Baryshnikov told Gold and Fizdale. "There's jokes about him. They say he had only two corrections: 'Don't fall!' and 'Get up!' Sometimes saying 'Don't fall!' at the right moment is worth more than detailed explanations of pyrotechnics. The timing of the class was extraordinary. It gets into you."

The single-minded concentration on developing classical technique during the teenage years is a feature at all great ballet academies geared to produce professional dancers at a relatively early age. A contemporary child psychologist, unfamiliar with and unsympathetic to the unrelenting demands of a system that insists there are only five possible positions for the feet to be in at any given time, would undoubtedly be horrified to witness the mental and physical straitjacketing that is a matter of everyday policy. Even in the West, where the state does not take on the official parenting of such gifted youngsters, the demands placed on ballet students seem awesome.

Baryshnikov's descriptions of his years under Pushkin are full of the agonies and satisfactions of total commitment. His reputation as a Lothario was not established here. If there were flirtations, they were all innocent. Life was strict, and the physical demands placed on all the students, every day, curtailed most extracurricular activities. Added to this was the fact that Pushkin quickly came to see in Baryshnikov the potential of the great star he eventually became. The teacher's commitment to

BARYSHNIKOV: A HOTEL ROOM WARM-UP

BARYSHNIKOV WATCHING HIMSELF ON TELEVISION

the pupil became total, and he and his wife emotionally adopted the boy and made an alternate home for him, a home Baryshnikov remembers with passionate affection. Most of all, Pushkin recognized that Baryshnikov's talent meant that he was going to have to fight very hard to transcend the automatic type-casting that was awaiting him in the rigid world of professional ballet in the Soviet Union.

"Pushkin always believed I would be a classical dancer, not a *demi-caractère*," Baryshnikov told Gold and Fizdale. "Nobody else thought so, because I was so tiny, with a baby face. But he said, 'Just keep going, keep going.' He gave me incredible love."

With Pushkin behind him, Baryshnikov kept going. His emergence onto the professional stage from the hothouse of Soviet ballet was ordained and unavoidable. He was required to compete, which he did with enthusiasm, in the crucially important Varna competition, where he won top honors in 1966 at the age of eighteen. Three years later he was the obvious choice for the gold medal at the Moscow International Ballet Competition, by which time he was already one of the fastest-rising stars in the Kirov Ballet.

The *annus mirabilis* in the second life Baryshnikov led in the Soviet Union was 1970. He fell in love with a fellow artist at the Kirov, Natalia Makarova, and got his first taste of the West during the company's famous visit to London. Although a few of the Western ballet cognoscenti had traveled to Leningrad and got wind of the fact that Pushkin had unveiled yet another protean talent, the London tour made by the Kirov was the first chance Western audiences and critics had to see the stage miracles Baryshnikov was capable of performing. Rudolf Nureyev was approaching the height of his remarkable and unquestioned mastery of the ballet stage, and despite the fact that Baryshnikov showed no sign whatever of the dramatic, brooding majesty the older Russian had built his fame around, the younger man was an instant sensation. It was his sheer technical prowess that left everyone's solar plexus so exhausted. There was nothing he seemed incapable of doing, and very shortly thereafter, the most adventurous dance critics—notably Arlene Croce in *The New Yorker* and Clement Crisp in *The Financial Times*—began speculating in print about the impact such an innovative technical genius could have on choreography itself. Once again defined as very special, Mikhail Baryshnikov began to be touted as one of those rare artists capable of extending the frontiers of his art.

Heady stuff indeed, especially since this is not a dancer who is oblivious to his notices. Neither did he remain oblivious to the hordes of beautiful ballet groupies ("bunnies," to use the in-house argot of the times) who clustered at the stage door, or the higher-class version of the same species, who had ways and means to get beyond the door itself. Baryshnikov began exploring the full effects of his stage appeal to women that year—spurred on, perhaps, by the fact that his intermittently requited love for the married Makarova came to a decisive conclusion with her own defection. It was on the 1970 trip that he met his American girlfriend, Christina Berlin, who was later able to visit him in Leningrad and was on hand in Canada when he defected there four years later.

The germ of an active plan to defect must have started here in London. Baryshnikov claims otherwise and stoutly maintains that the actual decision was only made definitively at the last possible moment, in Toronto. That is probably true on one level, since dreams and actions rarely meet. Subliminally, though, the road to the West had been building for some time, and to understand this it is necessary to see clearly what his life was like in the Soviet Union, unclouded by either the haze of anti-Soviet propaganda in the West or the facile nonsense spoken by the self-preserving Soviet elite.

The unvarnished truth is that Mikhail Baryshnikov had a very good life in Leningrad, a life happily encumbered by apolitical success and most of the little luxuries that such a success, in such a place, automatically brought. It may be, as Natalia Makarova has said, that the window to the West opened up by Peter the Great when he created the city that is now called Leningrad always has a beckoning effect on those looking out through it, but if Baryshnikov had been less of a rebel and less of an artist, there would have been no need for him to take the leap. He did not lack for travel, for women, for a handsome apartment in a former palace complete with housekeeper, for automobiles, or for a sense of accomplishment within the parameters established by his native land.

What he did lack, however, were mostly intangible things. On a personal, professional level, he had to live with the fact that as a relatively short and small dancer he was not considered suitable for many of the greatest classical male roles in the repertoire, such as the Prince in *The Sleeping Beauty* and his cousin in *Swan Lake*. This was deeply offensive not only to his aroused sense of self-esteem, but also to his intelligence and the vision of a comprehensive and great classical dancer sketched out for him by Pushkin. Also, well before he defected, he had had a taste of the kind of collaboration possible between a great dancer and a choreographer who could build works around an unfathomed potential.

Contemporary Soviet choreography is, by and large, plodding, but it does have some quirky masters, of whom the most impressive during Baryshnikov's days at the Kirov was Leonid Yakobson, who created for him an extraordinary solo dance entitled *Vestris*. It was upon this singular work that Baryshnikov rode to initial fame in the Soviet Union and at international competitions. The dance depicted the life of the famous French dancer and teacher Auguste Vestris (1760–1842), and Yakobson, famed for the delight he took in sending dancers on acrobatic fantasies, not only took the measure of Baryshnikov's buoyant athleticism, but may have been the first to gauge accurately the young dancer's natural skills as an actor and mimic.

Even given the limitations of Soviet choreography, Baryshnikov became the inspiration for the title role in Konstantin Sergeyev's *Hamlet* (1970), and Adam in *The Creation of the World* (1971) by Natalia Kasatkina and Vladimir Vasiliev. Here, however, the suspicion arises that the choreographers were attempting to latch on to the rising fame of the young dancer more than that they had anything exciting or new to say in their works. In any event it wasn't enough, and the stultifying artistic atmosphere, which dictated both the kinds of roles he was deemed suitable for and his inability to go exploring in ballet in ways that genuinely challenged him, bred within Baryshnikov a pervasive resentment that was bound to come out one day.

These were the sorts of things he would discuss with his closest friends, and in the Soviet Union friendship is a much more passionate and complicated affair than equivalent relationships in the West. To a trusted friend, a Russian can tell many things—but not everything. Yet he can share an intensity of emotional attachment that might strike us in the West as extreme and even predatory, because it is hard for us to understand the degree to which anxieties and cautious ambitions are communally held in Russia. We are good at quick friendships in the West—certainly in America—but less adept than Russians at giving those friendships genuine depth. If and when we do embrace "deep friendships," they often come with all the distressing embellishments of exposing ourselves and our psyches too much. Lacking editorial restraint, we let it *all* hang out.

Baryshnikov's well-developed skills at largely masking his true thoughts and emotions, not at all unusual in countries that seek to monitor and control precisely those same thoughts and emotions, eventually paid the kind of dividend he needed. He and his reigning favorite partner at the Kirov, Irina Kolpakova, were invited in the late spring of 1974 to front a provincial ragtag of dancers whom the Soviet cultural authorities, in one of their endless little cheats, were pleased to call the Bolshoi Ballet. By any standards, it was not what you would call a gilt-edged tour: The highlight was to be Canada, followed by a succession of two- or three-night stands in five countries in Central America. Still, it was a trip out of the Soviet Union, and there was keen competition among many dancers to join in.

The Canadian segment of the tour, begun in the small capital city of Ottawa, was to proceed to Montreal and Toronto and so on right out to Vancouver and down to Central America, neatly bypassing the one country everybody wanted to see. All the planning, all the brooding about consequences, all the pent-up anger of what had gone on before, and all the inchoate expectations of what was yet to come conspired together to help Baryshnikov bolt the unlovely embrace of his touring countrymen. Yet those last words he heard from the KGB minders on duty at the O'Keefe Centre in Toronto, as he ran through a parking lot to the appointed rendezvous, seemed to carry a subtext that would come to haunt him for several years: "Misha, Misha! Where are you going?"

It was a good question. The rendezvous completed, the safe house found, and a dozen toasts to freedom concluded, the morning after inevitably came and with it the realization of what a monumental step he had taken. A Russian mood descended. Husbands and wives sometimes go through the same thing the morning after their wedding; so do first-time house buyers upon signing the mortgage papers that leave them in debt for a quarter of a century. It was not the doubts of the heart or imminent penury that gnawed away at Mikhail Baryshnikov's soul the morning after, but the unalterable, unclear reality that one life had abruptly ended and another was about to begin.

So much has happened to him since those days that it is almost impossible to recall how modest were Mikhail Baryshnikov's specific expectations then and how genuine were his doubts and fears. In retrospect, they all seem laughable now. Would he be resented? Would his style be dismissed

BARYSHNIKOV IN NEW YORK

BARYSHNIKOV

as old-fashioned? Was his decision to defect premature? If he knew he was special, and he did, he was also vaguely aware that he was a product of a system—both professional and political—that had inculcated within him a self-disdain when he contemplated any aspiration beyond his particular specialty. And even within that specialty, despite his teacher Pushkin's admonitions, he was merely a category: a technical wizard, to be sure, but limited in both his dramatic scope and the variety of roles he could command.

Looking at him today, the most renowned male dancer of his generation and perhaps the most brilliant technician ever, artistic director of one of the foremost ballet companies in the world, and an outsized public personality who has been accorded American superstar status, it is clear that all these things were in his presiding star, which, as a true child of fate, he followed wherever it led. This, however, is only clear in retrospect. In the estate outside Toronto where he had been spirited away, his immediate concern was to get attached to a major ballet company—and detached from the first of the many female liaisons he forged so effortlessly with beautiful women in the West. For Christina Berlin, the daughter of the Hearst Corporation executive who thought she had walked into a fairy tale come true, things just didn't work out and she became the first woman on this side of the Iron Curtain who had to learn to separate the real Baryshnikov from the world of fantasy.

Very early after his defection the decision was taken to join American Ballet Theatre in New York. The company, with its dependence on the extravagant fame of foreign artists and a repertoire with which Baryshnikov was familiar, was a natural home base. A date was fixed for an American debut with Natalia Makarova on July 27, and it was a predictable triumph, complete with a glittering party afterward in the first of many Park Avenue penthouses he would come to know intimately. Jacqueline Onassis and her daughter, Caroline Kennedy, both came to look him over. So did Robert Massie, the author of *Nicholas and Alexandra* and *Peter the Great*, and Paul Newman and Joanne Woodward. Walking into this gold-flecked dream, however, was a young man who spoke virtually no English and spent the better part of the evening in a bedroom looking at old photographs from Russia.

"The phantom of Russia pursued and haunted me like a hangman," Baryshnikov told a Russian friend some time later about his first two years in America. "It [the phantom] was always invisibly watching my steps and made my life almost unbearable."

He grasped the only logical solution to keeping the phantom at bay, which conveniently also happened to coincide with his reasons for defecting. By throwing himself, almost maniacally, into his work, he used his first three years in the West to expand his range and repertoire as no artist in ballet had ever done before. There was virtually nothing he would not try, and no choreographer of rank he did not want to dress in his own persona: Antony Tudor, George Balanchine, Jerome Robbins, Roland Petit, John Butler, Twyla Tharp, John Neumeier—almost anything that was going by, he latched on to. His appetite for new dance was voracious, and tired only those who tried to keep up with him. In the process he became the most accessible ballet superstar in American history, performing regularly in New York and around the United States. He built up his own audience, one that could count on seeing him regularly and who would provide a solid foundation for a much wider array of fans who would rally to his banner through the ensuing decade. Critics responded with enthusiasm, and why not? The excitement he was generating meant that their own calling and their specific columns were also getting a wider audience.

During these three first years in the West, Baryshnikov also provided clear evidence of his penchant for disregarding what was expected of him and launching out into areas wiser minds warned him to avoid. This was part of his motivation for embracing the contemporary choreography of Twyla Tharp. Although many people were incredulous that he wanted to work with anyone so avant-garde, Baryshnikov's collaboration with her may have been his most important artistic leap since coming to the West, and the equal of his collaboration with Jerome Robbins. In his private life, too, he bucked up against people who assumed they could run his affairs without recourse to his own wishes and ambitions. As with his love affairs, there were untidy scenes as he struggled mightily to be freed from the prison of language. As his English improved, so also did the dismay of many people who thought they knew this man, only to discover that he turned out to be someone with a normal portion of complications, cultural misunderstandings, intolerance, secretiveness, bravado, chauvinism, and anger. A large part of Gelsey Kirkland's problem in the relationship the two dancers had made was her ability to fantasize what she thought it was all about and her inability to adjust to the emerging, and voluble, reality.

In 1978, Mikhail Baryshnikov made what is still considered the major controversial decision of his career. He cut his ties with ABT and moved over into the camp of the company's archrival: George Balanchine's New York City Ballet. For Baryshnikov, the move made perfect sense. He had been allowed only a sample of the Balanchine style at ABT, and he was aching to embrace it whole. Yet many of his admirers were aghast. While acknowledging Balanchine's genius, they also postulated that the acerbic choreographer downgraded the whole idea of superstars (except, it was archly pointed out, for himself) and expected all his dancers to play supporting roles to the choreography. To many, it seemed that in casting his lot with his fellow Russian, Baryshnikov was "trying to bury his own virtuosity."

For the star himself, who attacked the NYCB repertoire with his accustomed frenzied energy, the logic was inescapable. He wanted to be close to Balanchine and he wanted to feel Balanchine choreography in his bones. He knew that there *were* star roles in the repertory, and difficult ones at that. He wanted to learn them all. He worked like a demon, although among Balanchine aficionados, Baryshnikov's heated, exuberant style—however much he tried to tone it down—was always vying with Balanchine's cool intentions. His efforts to humanize the title role in *Apollo*, for example, were not appreciated, and such words as "impetuosity" and "self-indulgent" started appearing in the lexicon of criticism about Baryshnikov.

Personally, he adored being around the great choreographer. After he had left the company and after Balanchine had died, Baryshnikov would still talk with fire in his eyes of the pleasures of merely being near him. This was not immediately true, however. Balanchine stripped Baryshnikov of a lot of his illusions about himself as a performer, in an effort to cleanse him of "superstar sloppiness," which was a catchall phrase covering both egotistical excesses and the younger Russian's undoubted crowd appeal. Balanchine may also have inadvertently passed on his own autocratic attitudes to running a company. In fairly short order, though, the two men forged a relationship not unlike the one Baryshnikov had had with Pushkin back in Leningrad. At Easter, the two went off to a Russian Orthodox church to attend the Mass, after which they went back to Balanchine's apartment for a long breakfast. They talked about everything under the sun—about dancing, about food, about Russia, about New York. About women.

The Balanchine period, which lasted about fifteen months, was very important to Baryshnikov, but it is hard to escape the conclusion that it was flawed in two substantial categories. The dancer's own manifest and dramatic stage presence was altered and, for some, diminished, while at the same time the extraordinary new demands made on his body and muscles by taking on so many ballets in an unfamiliar style, meant that he had to push—and punish—himself far harder than he should have at this mature period of his career. He sustained some problem injuries and has been physically paying for the Balanchine period ever since.

After two seasons, Baryshnikov returned to American Ballet Theatre to succeed Lucia Chase as artistic director. Balanchine paid him a quintessentially tart tribute: "I would say Baryshnikov knows how to dance. He is intelligent and he has skill. He came and he learned. That is what he wanted."

He was also a wiser artist than when he had left Ballet Theatre, but the fervor of his enthusiasm had not dimmed, and he threw himself into new roles with the same degree of fanaticism that is the hallmark of his life as a professional dancer. He began pushing out into the world of American popular entertainment, the first taste of which had come in 1977, when he made the film *The Turning Point*. These forays distressed some of his colleagues no end. They could not understand why such a great classical artist wanted to sully himself with the taint of Hollywood or Broadway. They did not know their man. They did not even know that the very fact of their distaste was itself a kind of goad.

After a serious knee injury in 1982, which condemned him to a season of inactivity, he made a major reevaluation of his career and set himself upon the course he maintains today: acceptance of the role of artistic director of American Ballet Theatre, fewer personal performances in classical ballets (complete retirement was strongly hinted at in various publications in 1987), increasing exploration of television and movies, and a not entirely coherent search for roots and structure in his private life. If a love affair with the film star Jessica Lange did not end in marriage or even domestic tranquillity, as many of his friends hoped it would, it did produce a daughter—a tiny lump of humanity who at her birth did more than anyone else to secure Baryshnikov's sense of place and belonging in America. Even here, though, the complications of his career—and the nature of the choices he has felt compelled to make—leave nothing unsullied. He did not make it to the hospital for his daughter's birth, because he was obliged to perform in Syracuse, New York. Mention of this will almost bring tears of frustration to his eyes as he tries to explain why he could not be at the hospital, although his daughter clearly doesn't hold it against him. Miss Lange, on the other hand, decamped long ago.

And his trial by fire at the onset of his artistic directorship of American Ballet Theatre is now part of ballet history. The announcement of his appointment was greeted by howls of rage both inside and outside the company. Some people suspected that he would bring in Balanchine-style neoclassicism and concepts of "pure dance" at the expense of ABT's traditionally eclectic range of repertory. Others bemoaned the handing over of a leading American arts institution to a foreigner. It was also a time when ABT was facing labor strife that ended in a company lockout—with all the attendant bitterness. The season at the Kennedy Center in Washington, D.C., was scrapped. It was a terrible ordeal, and all around him people were ascribing to him dark plots and sinister motivations. He was forever, it seemed, trying to walk away from a myth that had nothing to do with him, but which clung tenaciously about him.

As it was in the Soviet Union, so it remains in the United States for Mikhail Baryshnikov. He does not quite fit in, and that is because his whole being is a mass of contradictions. An undeniable and healthy-sized ego is constantly undermined by his capacity for self-mockery and astonishing humility. A definitive and occasionally ostentatious affection for expensive things and for very rich people regularly jars with a relentless search for solitude and simplicity. One of his closest friends, the Nobel laureate poet and author Joseph Brodsky, loathes classical ballet with passionate vehemence, and Baryshnikov seems to love him for it. Brodsky, when chided about this, will even mount an argument that Baryshnikov himself hates being a dancer. "He despises himself for being a dancer," Brodsky will tell people. "He considers his body a machine, something apart from himself." Once, though, during the 1986–1987 season, Brodsky actually deigned to come to the Metropolitan Opera House in New York to see ABT perform some sparkling contemporary works. During the intermission Baryshnikov waited nervously for his friend to join him in the lobby.

"You see, Joseph," he said with all the disingenuous trepidation of a first-year law student tackling an aloof dean, "it's not all tutus and fluff."

And yet it is to this very world of tutus and perceived fluff that Mikhail Baryshnikov has dedicated so much of his life. This sense of his being an outsider inside his own world, which complicates his role as an artistic director in both predictable and unexpected ways, is reinforced by the fact that he still carries around within him a great deal of his boyhood and adolescence: in his career as an artist unsatisfied with established practice, in his attitude to everyday life, in his search for parental substitutes, in his ambivalent embrace of commitments, and even in his very physical demeanor. Despite those aching, damaged bones—talismans of encroaching middle age and a punishing career—he still leaves the strong impression that the prime of Mikhail Baryshnikov has not yet been reached.

SIR KENNETH MACMILLAN

TRUE HEIRS

*T*he ballet company Mikhail Baryshnikov presides over is fleshed out for the most part by dancers half his age, many of whom made their crucial decision to dedicate themselves to this arduous and often unyielding art after being inspired by a vision of him during their even younger days. Thereby hangs a tale or two. Any contemporary Rip van Winkle who had seen American Ballet Theatre fifteen years ago and reawakened yesterday to its current incarnation would scarcely believe his eyes. Baryshnikov first danced with ABT in 1974, when he was exactly the sort of imported novelty item that the company was notorious for contracting and which New York audiences still adore. Today, even if he is physically willing, he rarely dances with his troupe and has set his company for the most part on a trajectory largely eschewing guest stars, that has been the source of extraordinary controversy, extended critical ire, and internal dissension. Yet nothing he has done in his life, except for his defection, has shown him more courageous or daring than this attempt to give his beloved new homeland a classical ballet system and style worthy of both his own extraordinary roots in Russia and what he perceives as the energy and dynamism of America. It has been a monumental gamble and this man is never happier, apparently, than when he is fighting the odds.

George Balanchine, of course, had effected his own brilliant and distinctive transformation of American ballet through the filter of his Russian sensitivity by creating a choreographic ethos and an entire body of work that extended and redefined the classical lexicon. But Mikhail Baryshnikov was never interested in becoming a choreographer, and he was after something quite different. He did not want a single, concentrated perspective; instead, he was searching for a clear, eloquent, and, above all, coherent style which acknowledged the supremacy of a technical tradition he understood to be the best. This, in turn, would give his company the key to all the classics, as well as a recognizably consistent solution to the entire gamut of new choreographic expressions exploding in America. He could not do it alone, and the chief instruments in this technical strategy were his principal ballet mistress, Elena Tchernichova, and the company's régisseur, Susan Jones. These two women had the often lonely task of turning the corps de ballet into a striking force for the new perspective—Jones in vetting new dancers and working on casting lists with Baryshnikov and Charles France; Tchernichova in drilling the corps, encouraging potential soloists, and acting as coach, psychologist, and mother-figure to the principal dancers chosen by Baryshnikov to champion the new style.

In making those choices among dancers, Baryshnikov embraced the cult of youth almost from his first full day as artistic director. He cut a swath through the bulky company repertoire and started featuring young dancers in trimmed-down, cool versions of the classics that were immediately disliked by most critics and much of the traditional ABT audience. "Since I'm running the company," he said at the time, "I'd like to see the dancers doing the ballets the way I think they should be done. That's why I'm here."

The critical verdict on where Baryshnikov has taken the old Ballet Theatre is still undecided, although the extraordinary initial controversy has gradually ebbed away. During the 1986–1987 performing season, opinion began finally tilting strongly in his direction, seven years after he took over the post of artistic director from Lucia Chase, who was one of the company's founders in 1939, and Oliver Smith, who had been co-director with Chase since 1945. That season was remarkable in many ways—beginning with the "encouraged" resignation of the most notable arbitrageur on the ABT board of trustees, Ivan Boesky, and concluding with a startling but nevertheless official invitation to Baryshnikov to return for a visit to the Soviet Union. In between, the company unveiled a sumptuous new production of *The Sleeping Beauty*, which stretched its resources and the endurance of its dancers to the limit—and beyond. It was precisely the sort of expensive production that has bankrupted famous companies in the past, and ABT has had to develop a comprehensive program of hard—and even crass—campaigns to raise money in large amounts to meet both the artistic demands and the expectations of audiences.

It was a season in which the "Baryshnikov ballerina" was to be formally featured, notably in the person of principal dancer Susan Jaffe, in a succession of classical and modern ballets. New choreography, including an important work by one of the company's own dancers, would embellish the notion of a company caught up in its own creativity while joyously committed to the traditions of the classical past. There were galas for public consumption and tragedies for private grief. And, as always with ABT, the usual assortment of scandals—real and otherwise—to titillate the public. Yet the greatest and least celebrated achievement of the season was the simple recognition from audiences, fund-raisers, and even most ballet critics that there appeared to be some method, and perhaps genius, in the apparent madness of avoiding the easy lure of the star system.

The star system, as it was practiced at ABT, had complex origins and was not easy to dismantle. The New York City Ballet, for example, with its emphasis on Balanchine's neoclassical works, has traditionally been thought of as "anti-star." In fact, not only was the choreographer himself a monumental star, but the company developed dancers like Melissa Hayden, Edward Villella, Suzanne Farrell, and Peter Martins, who were certainly regarded as stars by New York audiences. ABT, on the other hand, had a major dependency on the famous nineteenth century classics such as *Swan Lake* and *Giselle* which—by their very nature—engendered stars. Moreover, because of this dependency, the stars themselves were able to wield extraordinary power over even the artistic staff. In the old days, if a prima ballerina was not of a mind to do something she had been asked, she simply didn't do it. Most of the broiling rows Mikhail Baryshnikov would have with Fernando Bujones during the first few years of his artistic directorship sprang from Bujones's assumption of old-style star prerogatives, which clashed directly with Baryshnikov's concept of developing a strong, cohesive, and unified dancing ensemble. Baryshnikov himself would say later that he was not against stars—and, indeed, he does still deploy them in the old-fashioned way for special galas, although they are rarely allowed to linger—but against "star self-indulgence." In reversing ABT's longtime dependency on stars, perhaps only the brightest star in the firmament could have led the way.

Certainly, what was at stake was no ordinary dance company. American Ballet Theatre, unprofitable as it may always be, is one of the most fascinating, intensely scrutinized, complicated, and multifaceted arts organizations in America. It is also one of the few remaining touring troupes in the world. Lots of large ballet companies do tour from time to time, but none is required to do so perpetually for the very sake of survival. Massively undersubsidized by government funding, unlike any of the famous or even modest ballet companies in Europe, American Ballet Theatre sets out several times each year for extended tours of the American hinterland that will see them away from their home base for as many as three months at a time, and a total of nearly six months out of the year. Although it is strongly identified among New Yorkers as the ballet company that dances at the Metropolitan Opera House at Lincoln Center, it is in effect no more than a seasonal tenant there, with preferential rights of access. The fact remains that American Ballet Theatre has no permanent performing home anywhere and has only recently acquired its own rehearsal and administration building in New York. And despite a comprehensive program of private fund-raising and often wildly successful New York seasons at the Met, after the season ends the company does not employ the dancers again until the return of the annual cycle—that is, if they get rehired.

New York is the dance capital of the world and has reigned supreme in that role for some time. Dancers' salaries have improved over the years at all levels, especially in the lower ranks, where corps members now make between $425 and $830 a week, compared to less than $300 seven years ago, while self-esteem has been hugely embellished by the so-called dance revolution which began in New York in the sixties and continued apace through the following decade. Even so, the stark fact remains that some dancers at one of the five top troupes in the world (the others being the Kirov in Leningrad, the Bolshoi in Moscow, the Royal in London, and the New York City Ballet) are required to go on the sanitized contemporary equivalent of the dole every year. If the prospect of collecting unemployment insurance is not sufficiently bleak, an ABT dancer can stoically contemplate the average span of his or her professional dancing days. It rarely lasts more than two decades, coming to an abrupt conclusion before the age of forty. If you are Fonteyn or Nureyev or Baryshnikov, you can dance forever, or at least as long as you can manage a creaky plié. If you are a conscientious but otherwise unnoticed member of the corps, you will find yourself relentlessly vetted by the artistic management for signs of wear and tear. Eventually, they will come for you and say: "Now, dear, I think you know as well as we do what this meeting is all about. . . ."

Each year, on the road or back at home in New York, Baryshnikov and his artistic staff hold regularly scheduled auditions for young dancers from all over America (all over the world, really). In some ways, they differ little from any other sort of auditions: many come calling, and extremely few are chosen. Just getting a chance to audition is something of an ordeal. The network of contacts between the artistic staff at ABT and all the well-known schools of ballet around the country is extensive. Many of the young people turning up for auditions have arrived on the specific recommendation of their teachers, who happen to have either a direct or indirect contact with one of the ballet masters or mistresses. If someone is touted as truly exceptional, and the person doing the touting has a proven record of talent development, he or she might get a private audition with Baryshnikov, but this is rare. For the most part they come in clutches on audition days, trying to pretend they aren't nervous, and hoping against hope that the years of hard work are finally going to pay off. They are numbered and noted in coldly clinical detail. After a basic technical competence is ascertained, decisions are sometimes made in seconds and based on pure whim, and the atmosphere is reminiscent of an animal auction.

In an odd and quieter way, though, auditions are an infinitely sad business because the demands of ballet are so much stricter and more rigorous than those of any other of the performing arts, while the return—even with success at the audition level—seems to outsiders so meager. Yet if the ballet world has its share of rebels, malcontents, and rational critics who all resent the "system" as it is presented to them, it is also remarkable for the broad and sublime rejection of common sense. Common sense would tell parents never to send their children to ballet school. Common sense would tell teenagers that there is a wider and happier world beyond the grueling strictures of daily barre and class. Common sense would tell the graduating student that there are infinitely superior ways of making money than joining a professional ballet company. Common sense would tell a young dancer that very few—laughably few—of his or her colleagues will ever make it to the top or even near the top. Common sense would tell a maturing dancer that there is much psychological grief stored up for his middle age and, quite often, great pain in old age.

Yet there remains the dance and dancers, and that fact alone testifies to the endurance of faith and sacrifice in an unbelieving age. There

SUSAN JONES WORKING WITH KATHLEEN MOORE

BONNIE MOORE AND JURGEN SCHNEIDER

JOHAN RENVALL AT ABT's HOME, 890 BROADWAY

MARTHA JOHNSON

AUDITION ASPIRANTS

BARYSHNIKOV OBSERVING AN AUDITION

ARTISTIC STAFF MEMBERS (*FROM LEFT*): BARYSHNIKOV,
CHARLES FRANCE, SUSAN JONES, DAVID RICHARDSON, FLORENCE PETTAN

BARYSHNIKOV

ASHLEY TUTTLE, ONE OF THOSE CHOSEN FOR THE COMPANY

BARYSHNIKOV

CENTER: LORA SMITH

FROM LEFT: GEORGINA PARKINSON, WENDY WALKER (*IN THE MIRROR*),
JOHN TARAS, BARYSHNIKOV, CHARLES FRANCE

GEORGINA PARKINSON

THE ARTISTIC STAFF DISCUSSING THE AUDITION

remains also American Ballet Theatre, where dancers laugh at the prospect of injuries which will almost surely come to them, somewhere, sometime. There remain the growing dance audiences, which measure the quality of life in the amount of time they are able to witness the ephemeral but always sacramental beauty of a body giving grace to unexpected dimensions. In the business of ennobling the human spirit, dancers offer us our only earthly chance to catch a glimpse of the angelic host. Uniquely, their contribution to the mystery of life comes through transcending the metaphysical and intellectual to demonstrate—neither with sonorous instruments nor with eloquent words, but merely with their own bodies—that the soul aspires to the highest ground.

Like the opera house in Bari, Italy, where ABT danced and filmed *Giselle* the previous autumn, the building at 890 Broadway near New York's Greenwich Village has about its exterior an air of shabby gentility. "The last studio space in Manhattan that is both affordable and suitable for the performing arts," as the company prospectus once called it, is jostled by greasy-spoon restaurants, down-market discount stores, and secondhand book emporiums. Yet it is home to American Ballet Theatre, a home with a difference because now the company has protected status there, thanks to the generosity of a farsighted patron who understood ABT's gathering sense of insecurity, an insecurity that directly arose from never knowing whether or not it was going to be booted out of yet another set of premises.

For all the economic hardships ABT has suffered over the years, it has also been the beneficiary of extraordinary philanthropy. Few have been so adroit as the remarkable Lawrence A. Wien, a New York real estate developer who finally resolved the half-century-old dilemma of a company that never owned the floor its dancers walked on. In 1986, when it looked as if ABT would have to vacate its premises yet again, Wien not only came up with a million-dollar deposit toward the $14.5 million purchase price of 890 Broadway, he vowed to finance the entire project with a low-interest mortgage and challenged the company and other occupants of the building to start a campaign to raise the $4.5 million remaining on the down payment.

Inside, the building has been cleverly renovated, and while it is far from luxurious there is a certain élan—albeit Spartan—which is the natural byproduct of sheer proprietorship. The building housing ABT's new home, which it shares with the Eliot Feld dance troupe, was built in two sections in 1896 and 1897 and began life as a department store in what was once the flourishing Union Square mercantile area. Something of the rambling atmosphere of its previous incarnation can still be felt as you roam its seemingly endless corridors. A wrong turn one way will bring you into a large studio where, depending on the time of day, most of the ABT dancers will be going through their daily warm-up exercises and ballet class, or rehearsing a scene from an upcoming production. Along the echoing corridors, the sound of endlessly unended piano music ricochets from wall to wall. More likely than not it is Gladys Celeste at the keyboard. Like Florence Pettan, Celeste has been at ABT "forever," having vacated the Philippines well before the Marcoses came to power. Also like Pettan, she carries within her memories of the old Ballet Theatre which tend to transcend all the comings and goings of the current crop of dancers and artistic staff. Even as she deals with the problems of the day, there is a sense with Gladys Celeste that she has seen it all before, many times over.

As Gladys and others churn out their ceaseless piano accompaniment, the mood of each daily class varies, depending on the ballet master or ballet mistress who is leading it. Elena Tchernichova, for example, tends to intrude to make corrections on very specific details, like arm positions and attitude. She saves her more exacting demands for smaller-scale sessions when she can talk through a problem with a dancer. Jurgen Schneider, on the other hand, feels no compunction about using sarcasm or black humor when he feels the need of it, and has something of the mien of an old-fashioned taskmaster, which is mostly bluff. Nearly all the dancers are there for class each day. The exceptions are notable. The veteran prima Martine van Hamel, along with a few of the other senior ballerinas, has her own very decided views on who can keep her properly in shape for the grueling sequence of rehearsals and performances, and she never comes to a general class—a source of habitual resentment on the part of some of the senior artistic staff.

Baryshnikov usually takes class with the company. He no longer goes full-out, although sometimes—if he is angry with himself or simply wants to remind someone he's still the lord of the dance—he will do amazing things after he is fully warmed up. At first sight he seems not to be paying much attention to his dancers, but after a while, if he's of a mood, he will make the rounds, offering opinions or even demonstrating a problem or a model move. There is near unanimous agreement within the company among those who have been around him more than two years that he has become more accessible as his own dancing career recedes into history. "He is generally very relaxed with us now," said a principal male dancer, who rolled his eyes when asked about Baryshnikov's earlier relationship with dancers in class. "And it is widely appreciated. Nearly everyone here would stab his mother in the back for one minute's worth of his attention. These days he's giving people more than a minute, and I think you can see the difference in the dancing, and you can certainly sense it in the overall morale."

There are many other curiosities to be observed at the daily class. Quite often, those working hardest—putting everything within them into their preparation and deployment—are not necessarily among the favored dancers. Johan Renvall, an interesting and important soloist with the company, is often found opting out on the sidelines, while John Gardner, another soloist, takes his need for class much more seriously and seems to work correspondingly harder than Renvall. It is fascinating to see how such a contrast works out in casting and performance. Renvall's appeal to the artistic staff is obvious when the curtain actually goes up. There's a menace, difficult to define, in his feline stage presence. Despite his apparent lack of endeavor in class, he can invest certain roles with an intensity of mood and physical prowess that is as disturbing as it is riveting.

Gardner, however, offers no such dramatically volatile complications in his stage persona. He has simple, clean-cut good looks that tend to become more nondescript the farther you are from the stage. Perhaps this is the reason he works so hard on his technical skills, compensating for a lack of stage mystique with a clean and wonderfully competent line in his danc- ing. During various performances of *The Sleeping Beauty,* both young men were assigned the gruesomely onerous Bluebird role, which offers pre- cious little opportunity for character development and exposes technique with relentless intensity. Although Renvall is considered the better dancer of the two in the comprehensive evaluation the artistic staff must make of a dancer's whole self-projection, he was clearly defeated by this role. An outsider might have attributed it to his lackluster performance in daily class; an insider—one of the ballet masters—attributed it to the high expectations aroused by the Bluebird role which daunted Renvall each night he was expected to dance into the mythology. Yet Gardner, while certainly not an exceptional virtuoso consistently danced the Bluebird far better than anyone else in the company and often enough saved this whole section of the crucial final act of *The Sleeping Beauty* from dwindling into an academic performance.

When the dancers who had accompanied Mikhail Baryshnikov to Bari returned to New York in mid-autumn, they had barely forty-eight hours to swap tales with those who had been left behind. Some of them must have been considerably annoyed at the way they were whisked out of Italy at the end of the shoot, because their ire was passed along the company grapevine and the bitter feelings of the months before were neutralized. "One good thing happened," said a sarcastic returning corps member. "There was no culture shock. How could there be? No one had a chance to see any culture."

With just two days to get over jet lag, these and the other company members had donned their rehearsal warm-up clothes and were hard at work at the onset of another ballet season: not the public season, but the real company season, which always begins with sweat and grind and, often enough, ends ten months later in fractured bones and torn ligaments. In between, of course, is all the power and glory.

The constituent parts of the American Ballet Theatre year—any year—are mostly known anywhere from eight to eighteen months in advance. If the major and costly decision has been taken to mount a new full-length production from the classical repertoire, some decisions have to be taken several years in advance. A guaranteed tour, a guaranteed season at the Metropolitan Opera House, guaranteed Christmas appearances with *The Nutcracker* in Los Angeles—these are counted on, planned for, and orchestrated in the company offices back in New York. Programming can be a nightmare, especially when Baryshnikov's own busy schedule has to be dovetailed into the company season.

For the 1986–1987 season, the decision had been taken in 1985 to mount a revival of some of the best-known works of Antony Tudor, the English-born choreographer who was in on the birth of Ballet Theatre and whose probing psychological works are so identified with the company by critics and dance historians. Tudor himself, as Baryshnikov and Charles France knew very well, had strong views on how his own ballets should be mounted. Despite his great age—and no one at the time was quite sure what that was, so that it became a debating point with his sudden death mid-season—Tudor himself was enlisted in the project. The company had to decide at which point during the Met season it would be appropriate to launch the Tudor revivals, and that specific moment had to be traced backward right through from the final dress rehearsals, individual coaching for dancers, costume fittings, set design and construction, and role assignments.

The new season had been fitted together with great precision by more than a dozen individuals in the company. On artistic matters—choice of repertoire, commissioning of new ballets, invitations to guest artists and choreographers, cast lists—Baryshnikov makes virtually all of the final decisions. He is quite straightforward in his approach, has strong views on all levels—on the various qualities of the dancers themselves, on decor, on the right mix of offerings during the season, and so on—and likes to gamble if things look a little too safe or conservative. On the other hand, it is also true that his staff has become adroit in making sure that his choices aren't too complicated. Régisseur Susan Jones does all of the spadework on the availability of dancers at a given time of year, and she has her own strong views on who would work best with what. Associate Director John Taras, who worked closely with George Balanchine at the New York City Ballet until the great choreographer's death, adopts a low-key and pragmatic role when giving Baryshnikov his views, but he offers the solidity of experience, which sometimes is crucial. The ringmaster in all this is Charles France, whose loyalty to Baryshnikov is legendary, and who—as a master of detail—is something of a genius at presenting well-defined choices to a man who can become bored and irritated by too many details. By far the most complex and controversial senior figure in American Ballet Theatre today, France is rarely given credit for being such a master of details. It is this very forceful character who is usually knocking down the doors of hospitals to get dancers immediate medical attention; it is France who went to bat for an AIDS victim and stayed the course till the end; and it is France who has to deal with parents or spouses of dancers when there are grievous personal problems. The list goes on and on, and the same man is required to reconcile conflicts on all levels of company activity—even those he himself causes, either directly or inadvertently.

All the rest of the company is eventually drawn into the decisions made by the artistic staff. The dancers themselves get their specific marching orders once they know the roles they have been assigned. Production personnel start planning the logistics of building sets that will stand up to the bruising national tour, while the wardrobe staff begin their detailed liaison with costume designers. While all this is going on, the company's promotion people are poking their noses into all the plans to see how much publicity mileage can be gained from new productions or special evenings during the season. Galas, for example, generate excitement, press coverage, and extra revenue. Mounting a gala is a major undertaking, involving the promotion people, led by the ebullient and committed Robert Pontarelli and Elena Gordon, who work with Director of Development Lawrence Lynn; volunteer organizations associated with the company, like the Friends of ABT; business sponsors; and as many members of the board of trustees and their corporate friends as can be cajoled into contributions and attendance.

The major challenge this season is the new production of *The Sleeping Beauty*, the greatest of the legend-laden classical ballets. It has been especially commissioned from ABT's new artistic associate, Sir Kenneth MacMillan—the former artistic director of Britain's Royal Ballet and still its principal choreographer—and before one step has been danced on opening night, it will have cost slightly over $1 million. This is an enormous investment, and much depends upon the ballet's success, because it will be expected to generate great performances, big audiences, and wide critical acceptance for the better part of a decade. A major production of one of the preeminent classics, if it is a hit, can linger on in repertoire even longer and be extremely remunerative. A major production that is a flop, or one that gets only a middling reaction and is doomed to die within a couple of years, is a major disaster. Much then rides on Sir Kenneth's creation. The production was set in New York and was ready to work on when the dancers returned from Bari. As the company crisscrossed America with the first part of the season's repertoire, ballet masters and ballet mistresses would take some principals and soloists off to polish the myriad intricate and difficult dances that make up *The Sleeping Beauty*. Finally, in Chicago—more than a month before the production was unveiled in New York on April 20, 1987—*The Sleeping Beauty* had its world premiere. "Tryout" is probably a more accurate description, but Chicago would have resented the phrase. The hope in all this was that by the time of the New York premiere, the company would have an acknowledged and sparkling jewel to show off.

*   *   *

As the season progresses and the dancers get increasingly tired and prone to greater stress and injury, Peter Marshall's life becomes hell.

Marshall is the company physical therapist. He is also Baryshnikov's personal therapist. Wearing both caps keeps him busy, particularly when the company is performing and he has to set up shop in whatever theater or hall ABT finds itself in. His little clinic never looks much different, whether it's at the Metropolitan Opera House or at the Kennedy Center in Washington, or lost somewhere within the hideously yawning cavity that is the Shrine Auditorium in Los Angeles, where the company dances each year for two seasons.

The little set of rooms at the Met is bleak and sterile. Although it has been fitted out with the portable paraphernalia of a temporary clinic, the difference in style between the Met's laundry room—which it is most of the year—and Peter Marshall's traveling bone-manipulating hospital—which it is during the American Ballet Theatre season at the Met—is minimal. The bodies frequenting the premises during the ABT season, of course, are more beautiful than those of the launderers. On the other hand, they are also in a lot deeper trouble. That is why they come to the room of sighs and groans. The dancers come and go from Marshall's premises in a steady stream, always by appointment unless there is an emergency.

Some of the dancers are very specific and clinical when they arrive. "Peter," said one who popped his head in the door, "I'm having real problems with my Achilles tendon. Sometimes it gets real painful and just gives way. It's got me scared."

Marshall, who was in the middle of what looked ominously like a half-nelson hold atop principal dancer Victor Barbee, frowned a bit as he pushed down harder on Barbee, who groaned. The therapist dislikes being interrupted and works hard to be patient.

"Well, an Achilles tendon can't really do that kind of thing," Marshall told the dancer at the door as he continued his assault on Barbee. "Come back in a bit. I'm all tied up right now."

In fact, the therapist wasn't at all tied up; that was the fate of Victor Barbee. "I don't want to talk about my problems, because they just get me depressed," said Barbee, blithely fibbing, because in truth he adores analyzing all his ailments. They are his children and he nurtures them with tender loving care. "I grew six inches in one year and I also had a, a, *aaargh* . . ." Marshall had apparently discovered a pertinent sore point.

Over in a corner, ABT's new hotshot boy wonder, Argentinian

PETER MARSHALL

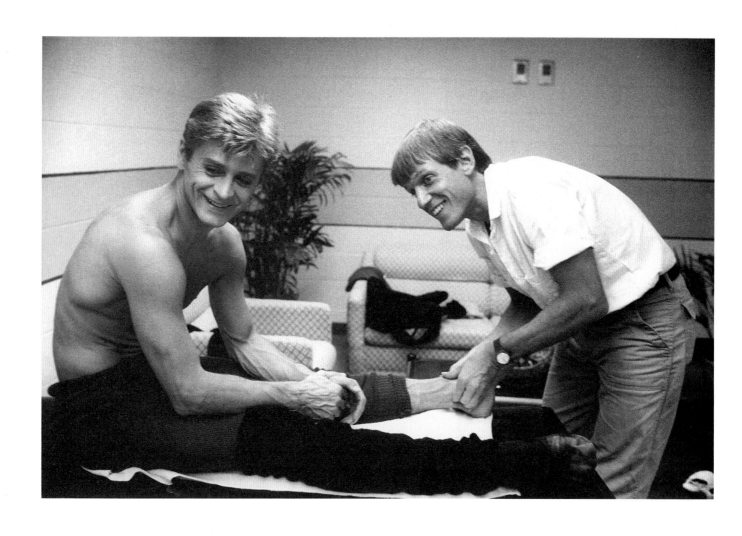

BARYSHNIKOV AND PETER MARSHALL

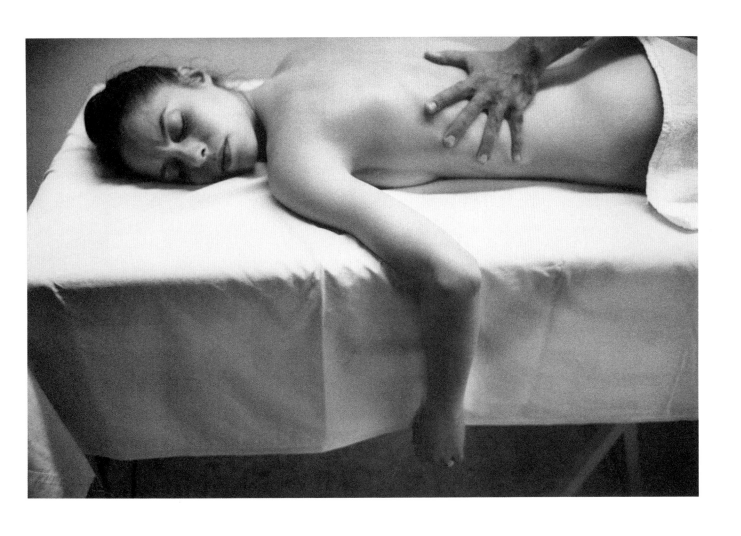

SUSAN JAFFE BEING MASSAGED BY RAYMOND SERRANO

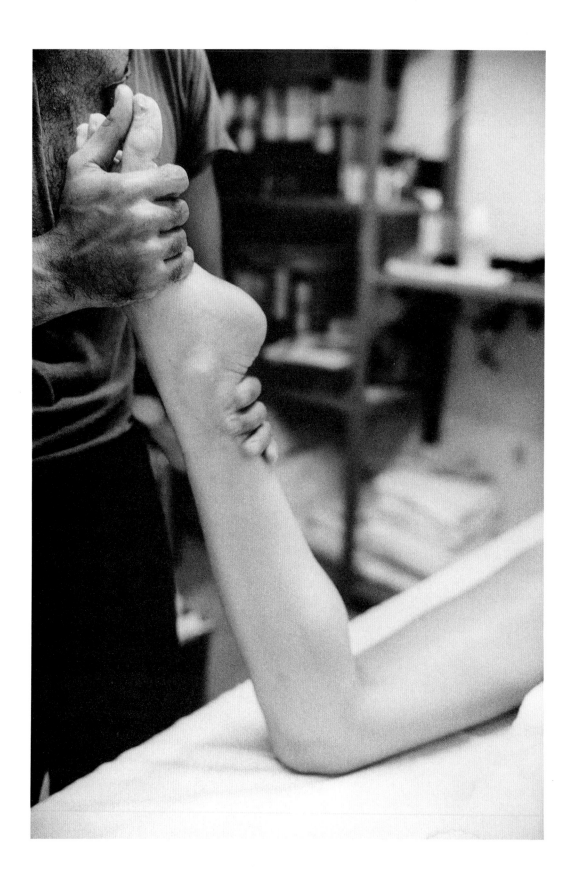

SUSAN JAFFE

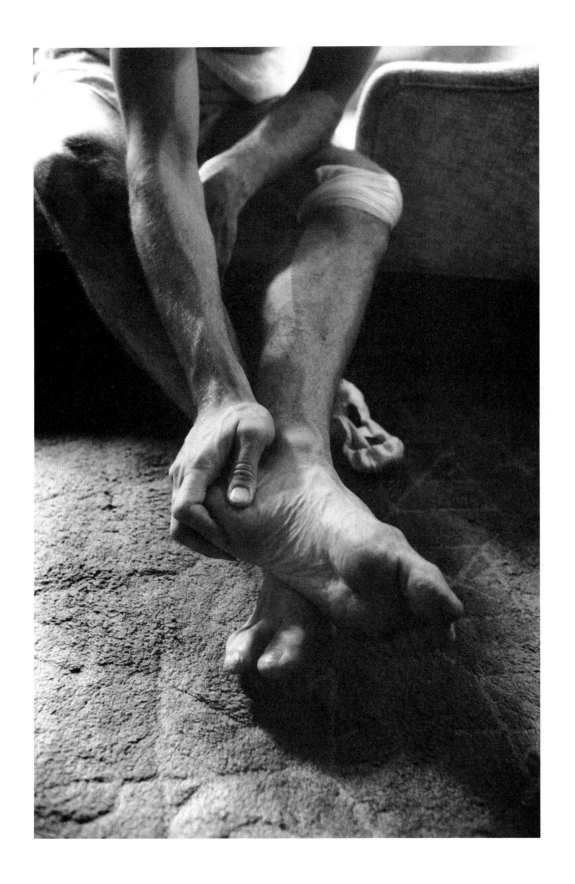

PATRICK BISSELL

principal dancer Julio Bocca, was sitting patiently on a bench as electrical therapy was being applied to the calf of a leg. He is not a groaner but a sigher, and his sighs are beautiful because he uses them as an alternative to the English language. When he sighs, his eyes roll heavenward and his careful smile hardly disturbs the distinctive features of his face. It is most affecting, and when you ask him the time of day or whether he has eaten yet, he sighs again and offers up a bit of his precious store of the local argot: "Is okay. Is okay." The most promising male of the new generation of dancers Baryshnikov has recruited during the past two years, Bocca came straight from Buenos Aires and has been singularly successful in resisting any effort to speak or understand English. Company members who speak Spanish, especially soloist Robert Hill, are his principal intermediaries. Bocca is very gifted and quick, although he is vain, and periodically is observed to be lazy. He remains perfectly oblivious to the palpable jealousy his precipitous rise through the ranks of the company has aroused. He may understand more than he lets on. If so, he is wise beyond his years.

Some dancers eschew Peter Marshall's clinic and regard it in much the same way that celibates do a house of ill repute. "Personally, I think Peter is very thoughtful and sincere," said Ty Granaroli, "and professionally I'm sure he is as competent as they come. But some of us feel his clinic has become something of a psychological crutch. I'm not talking about genuine cases, but the dancers who like to be constantly fussed over and nurture their little aches to satisfy their need for attention. Well, maybe that's too much pop psychology. Certainly something keeps drawing them back to Peter, and it sure isn't any serious physical disability."

It's probably true, in part. Dancers are suckers for the services and blandishments of acupuncturists, chiropractors, exotic herbalists, Eastern exercisers, and probably faith healers as well. When the company arrives in yet another town or city on tour, the calling cards of this feisty, mantra-spouting tribe go up on the notice boards near the stage entrance. If one of their number actually effects a cure or even an improvement, there is almost no limit to the strength of the business he or she can do during the remaining stay. In ancient days, they might well have been elevated to minor deities.

Marshall, typically, is tight-lipped about all this. He has reputable degrees and diplomas, a conservative private practice, and has even done front-line service trying to isolate welfare fraud cases, people who are looking for a lifetime-disability certificate. There are not many dancers who can fool Peter Marshall, although a few always try. He takes all his tasks very seriously, and nothing leaves him so troubled as a dancer—and there was one during the 1986–1987 season—whose tenuous psychological balance is manifested by imagined injuries. During every performance, Marshall can often be found in the wings watching his problem cases perform. He looks at their technique to spot clues to recurring ailments. He will even talk to them the moment they dart into the wings from the stage, and grill them about how they feel. Some appreciate it enormously; others resent it deeply. The therapist is seemingly oblivious to either sentiment. "I just try to keep people dancing," he says.

If the dancers, whatever their physical frailties, occupy the high ground of ballet, Larry Lynn must rake the low ground. As the chief money-grubber for a perpetually insolvent arts organization, Lynn—his official title is director of development—and his staff are responsible for coming up with all the business sponsorship programs and other incongruous circuses that often enough mean the difference between survival and extinction for American Ballet Theatre. He will grub for 2,500 dollars' worth of free Kleenex tissues from Kimberly-Clark to soak up the sweat of dancers' brows. He will grub for free champagne at a society ballet gala, where people encumbered with too much capital ever to make it through the eye of a needle may yet be induced to cough up $5,000 to keep one ballerina in toe shoes for a year. He will salivate for Merrill Lynch and the Movado Watch Corporation if they will underwrite part of a national tour. What he would do for a corporation that would rocket his own annual budget of around $5 million into an eight-digit trajectory is not known, but the imagination does not produce a pretty picture.

The official rundown of Lynn's "Responsibilities" begins pianissimo:

- Direct a $5.5 million Annual Campaign and a six year $50 million Golden Anniversary Campaign.
- Manage a Development department of 15 staff members with professionals specializing in such areas as corporate and foundation giving, direct mail, special events, patron programs, national membership, capital campaigns, and philanthropic earned income.
- Mastermind the fund raising efforts of a Board of Trustees

composed of 35 prominent corporate, social, and philanthropic leaders.
- Develop all recruitment tactics and objectives for the Board's Nominating Committee.
- Strategize and personally direct all major gift solicitations.
- Represent American Ballet Theatre publicly, especially in the corporate giving community.

It is under the "Accomplishments" section of his curriculum vitae, however, that the Larry Lynn engine of achievement gathers full steam:

- Since I arrived, private sector support for the Annual fund has increased from $2 million to $4.7 million.
- I targeted and guided the recruitment of 17 of the current 34 Board members, including four members of the Forbes 400.
- I have developed corporate sponsorship and direct mail programs that are considered among the finest in the performing arts community.
- Revenue from ABT galas and special events has increased 125% under my direction. The events have attracted social, political, business and entertainment industry notables across the country.
- I organized and wrote ABT's first long range strategic planning documents.
- I lobbied for, and successfully launched, ABT's first long-range capitalization . . .

Enough! Enough!

ABT on stage is one thing; ABT on the hustle is quite another. Larry Lynn, as his résumé proclaims, is clearly a modern miracle. The gnawing, stark reality in all this relentless self-assertion, however, is that ABT benefits greatly from Lynn's incessant pitch, despite the fact that it drives some people in the company right up the wall. He is not so much a fund-raiser as a corporate zealot and missionary who knows that he, or someone exactly like him, makes it possible for dancers to dance in a financially complicated modern world. It is surely a libel against his best instincts that he once explored the possibility of embroidering the Merrill

Lynch bull insignia on each and every ballerina's tutu. (The logical place-ment on male tights was apparently never discussed.)

Like most arts organizations, this company is constantly finding itself in deficit. It began its 1985–1986 season, for example, $2.4 million in the hole. Naturally, the company looks first and foremost to its wealthy board of trustees for direct tangible help. Each of the thirty-five trustees is theoretically under a moral obligation to come up with $100,000 a year, whether donated, raised, or coughed up personally. That's a theory. Ivan Boesky, before his precipitous departure, discovered a rather clever way to make a major commitment and hold on to his pennies. The Great Arbitrageur promised to underwrite the cost of a specially commissioned ballet focusing on the Holocaust. It is not clear whether this breakthrough of an idea was ever taken seriously—no choreographer was approached for this project—but it is impossible not to admire Boesky's brilliance in fending off the ever-importuning Lawrence Lynn.

The man is not loved among the artistic staff, and—off the record—he has his own views on the artistic staff's higher commitment to the exigen-cies of fund-raising. Still, they are officially required to get along with each other, and ever since Lynn arrived at ABT in 1979, the uneasy tension between art and the necessity of coming up with providential lucre has never been allowed to get out of hand, for the simple reason that no one can afford such a rupture. Government grants, which total around $1 million annually, are no longer adjusted for inflation, nor are they revised upward at all. Ticket sales are counted on to cover close to three quarters of ABT's annual operating budget of around $17 million. Lynn has to come up with the rest.

Charles Dillingham is the executive director of American Ballet The-atre, a position he rose to in 1984 after three years as general manager. Apart from his specific duties—overseeing the company's annual budget and supervising the overall administration—his key role is as a bridge between the board of trustees and the company itself, particularly the artistic staff. It would not be accurate to describe this key role as one that is mutually appreciated; the artistic staff often resents Dillingham, as it does Larry Lynn. Sometimes when the cool, buttoned-down Dillingham ambles onto a stage before the curtain goes up, in his Guccis and well-tailored dark suit—looking for all the world like the Inquistor General in a communal cell of heretics—sparks can fly.

Where Baryshnikov is all heat and passion and exclamation, Dillingham can seem militantly calm, somber, and waspish. Each appears to have decided he has the measure of the other, and they retain just that little edge of caution in their mutual relations that allows them both to get on with the job. Once, when Dillingham cajoled Baryshnikov into making an appearance before the board of the National Endowment for the Arts, there was bickering and complaining from the Russian almost up to the portals of the board room. "He performed just fine," said Dillingham, "but on the way there he told me exactly how he felt. 'I'd rather go to the dentist,' he said. And I believed him. I wouldn't describe him as an enthusiastic fund-raiser, but he does his duty and when he does it, he does it well."

Larry Lynn put it another way: "Look. I won't try and fool you by saying I think getting Misha to do anything at our end is easy. Frankly, it's damn difficult. He just hates doing that sort of thing. But he will do some, and I can tell you that two minutes of his presence anywhere will do more good than a whole year of glad-handing by any other artistic director in the country."

By declining even a penny of salary for his services as artistic director—a decision he made several years ago, in order to be formally rid of most of the obligations and demands which would inevitably be placed on him by Dillingham, Lynn, and the board if he was taking a normal salary—Baryshnikov appears to have won the right to tell his hierarchy to get stuffed if he doesn't want to do something: like dancing during the season, or doing a soft-shoe shuffle for the latest scheme Larry Lynn has dreamed up. The attitude sounds negative, but in fact it is just common sense and is the only way he can make his deeply compartmentalized life work. In his own mind, his life as a superstar—and the rewards that accrue from this status—are his own business, literally and figuratively. He exploits his own image on television and in film, in product endorsements and public appearances. No one is using him, and he makes his own decisions as to what is appropriate for him to do. His personal agent, the elegant and prestigious Edgar Vincent, handles many of his non-ABT activities, including tours and television contracts, and Charles France does his level best to straddle the two worlds to help avoid conflicts and contradictions. When Baryshnikov is with ABT, he gives his version of his all. Often the effort is superhuman; sometimes it is far less than most people want. His view is that at his company he is the artistic director and his obligations are to the dancers and his art. His superstar status is peripheral, and he resents the company management's trying to mine it. In a complicated attitude toward ABT, he seems both to love it and to resent the ties that bind him so closely to so many people's livelihoods. Yet he tarries there, and in the end, when he decides yet again not to bolt away, it is always because of the dancers and their expectations of him. It is certainly not to keep Charles Dillingham happy.

For his own part, Dillingham does not leave the impression that he is much bothered by the games that dancers or artistic directors play. He is what is known these days as a focused administrator, and for him the focus is on the perpetual lack of money his company always faces, a problem compounded in his mind by the want of a permanent theatrical home in New York City, which obliges ABT to remain on its exhausting touring schedule. Still, he was reasonably effusive—for him—as the 1986–1987 season was coming to a close. He was crowing about the major coup ABT had pulled off by getting a three-year agreement with the dancers six months before the current contract was up. The company had just announced that advance sales of tickets for the Metropolitan Opera House season were the largest in its history (around $5 million) with a 12 percent increase in the number of New York subscribers (to 13,700). And his wife had just given birth to a baby girl. All this allowed him a certain measure of distance from any little frictions with the artistic staff. Even on lesser matters he remained sanguine, especially on the disputatious subject of negative critical notices, a subject on which he finds Baryshnikov sometimes at the frontier of hysteria.

"Oh, he [Baryshnikov] overreacted to some negative reviews from the Los Angeles critics at our last board meeting," said Dillingham. "I wish he hadn't. Our audiences there are so broad and encompass so many people, the critics are largely irrelevant, and this talk just gets some members of the board in an unnecessary state."

At the same meeting, and subsequently, Baryshnikov would counter by complaining that the over-budgeting of the company's ticket sales in Los Angeles and the over-long seasons there, set against the lack of support from local critics, would result in bad box office figures the following year. And he was right, which didn't help the relationship between the artistic director and the executive director.

Charles Dillingham fusses about his board of trustees because its members are pivotal to his own job. He is also fairly blunt about what he expects from them:

"A change in attitude on the board began in the late sixties. There was pressure on the company to run its affairs more like a business, and that's what we do, although we try hard not to cut all costs to the bone. . . . The chief function of a board member is fund-raising, and the current board accepts that challenge well. We don't make any secret why we want someone on the board, and because of this it sometimes makes finding the appropriate person difficult. On the other hand, it certainly avoids getting dilettantes who prefer giving advice to money."

Although the opening night of ABT's season at the Metropolitan Opera House comes in the middle of the company's performing year, it is the unchallenged apex. In 1987, opening night was a mighty gala to celebrate the New York premiere of the new production of *The Sleeping Beauty*. Preceded by endless speculation in society and gossip columns, the evening was also intensely scrutinized by dozens of dance critics, who represent nearly the entire range of dance journalism in the United States, making this cultural event one of the most important of the year in America. Stars are born and reputations can lose their gloss in one night, but there is no denying the extraordinary atmosphere created. A lot of that atmosphere is stage-managed by the committee that arranges the gala, and whose business it is to ensure as high a profile for the event as is possible.

On April 20, despite all the nervous tummies backstage before the curtain opened, the real sparks were flying out front in the foyers and mezzanines of the Metropolitan Opera House, because Nan Kempner was angry as hell and wasn't about to take it anymore. Mrs. Kempner is not just another society lady around ABT; she is the high priestess of a "directed arts function" at which Larry Lynn is merely an altar boy. Appointed chairman, months before, of ABT's opening night gala at the Met, she decided to stage "a real man-pleaser" of an event to create the right atmosphere for the busy corporate and personal VIPs whom the company wanted to hit for donations. The whole gala bash was paid for by the Movado Watch Corporation and Moët-Hennessy, and Mrs. Kempner figured none of her worthy gentlemen who had coughed up from $500 to $1,250 per gala ticket would care for the usual four-course, postperformance banquet which kept people up until after 1:00 A.M. Instead, she conceived the idea of offering up-market, black-tie cocktail parties—catered by Mortimer's, the hot Upper East Side restaurant—built around the two intermissions in *The Sleeping Beauty*. In this way, "everyone would be home, happy and contented, by midnight."

And that's the way Kempner arranged it before she made the mistake of going to Europe a few weeks before the opening night. It was only upon her return that she discovered the altar boy and his friends at ABT felt people who had paid so much money might feel cheated with cocktail fare. The traditional banquet was reinstated in Kempner's absence.

No unwelcome intruder in a henhouse has ever caused as much squawking as Kempner did upon her return. She marched the evening's sponsors and the ABT management up the hill and down again and all around the circle. She announced her resignation from the board of trustees and generally complained so loudly and bitterly that a bizarre compromise was reached: Gala patrons would have a choice of Nan's cocktail parties or ABT's dinner. Nothing that happened onstage that night equaled the hype of Nan Kempner's little brouhaha. When asked whether he was going to partake of Nan's "tidbits" or Larry's "four-courser," Mikhail Baryshnikov assumed Don Quixote's doleful countenance and mumbled something about having to go to both. He looked and sounded for all the world like the turkey who was asked to say grace before Thanksgiving dinner.

It is not, however, for galas, opening nights, rave reviews, or funless fund-raising parties that dancers dance. They do so because, by the time they reach a company of the stature of Ballet Theatre, they can do nothing else. Their bodies and their minds have become so intertwined in the business of dancing and the evocation of fantasy that any farther reality falls out of focus. If *The Sleeping Beauty* is a great test for ballerinas on all levels, it is equally true that some fail—on all levels. Greet Vinckier, a hauntingly beautiful Belgian dancer in the corps, evidently failed during one performance at the Met—or, at least, she failed in her own estimation. Why she thought so was never clear because no one else had spotted any problems. The only thing that was obvious, as she walked toward a distant exit in the bowels of the Met's backstage area, far from the dancers' usual point of departure, was that she wanted to be alone. She didn't want sympathy either. She wanted anonymity. She wanted forgetfulness. The last person she wanted to meet was Mikhail Baryshnikov, who nevertheless came bounding along the same out-of-the-way corridor, keen to get his hands on his latest toy. A top-of-the-line Jeep Cherokee, all plush velour and leather inside, with all the engine trimmings under the hood, it was parked in a remote internal bay at the Met.

He passed her by at first, not seeing who she was, and then he turned and smiled. "It went okay tonight," he said, flashing one of those smiles of his which can light up the universe. That was when the tears came rolling down her cheeks.

"Greet, Greet. What's the matter?" he demanded.

"I danced so badly," she said, and lowered her head to avoid his gaze.

"Oh, no. Not so bad, not so bad. Don't be sad. It was okay tonight."

But she just kept her head lowered and passed him by.

He stood still and watched her walk away. After what seemed an age, he turned to his companion and said, "Let's go home. Wait till you see my fancy truck!"

Within a minute of midnight, he eased out onto Amsterdam Avenue and would have floored the accelerator if the light ahead hadn't turned amber. As he brought the vehicle to a stop, a high-pitched voice screeched *"Misha! Misha!"*

"My God," Baryshnikov said as he eyed the rearview mirror suspiciously. "What is this?"

Running out into the middle of the street and causing one car to swerve out of her path came a tall young Hispanic woman wearing high white boots, a short skirt, and a white leather jacket. She was holding a camera high up in the air. *"Misha!* I've waited so long to take your picture," she said when she finally caught up to the Jeep. "Oh, please, let me take your picture."

She was beautiful, and he is not oblivious to a woman's beauty, but the reason he rolled down his window and let her take a couple of flash pictures probably had more to do with the bizarre effect of her wild run down the middle of a busy avenue.

"Be careful," he said when she had finished taking her pictures. "I won't drive away until you get back to the sidewalk."

She couldn't move, so transfixed had she become by her close physical proximity to a presiding fantasy in her life. She just kept moaning, "Misha, Misha. Misha, you are beautiful. You are beautiful."

"Come on," said Baryshnikov sharply, realizing that the traffic around them was getting potentially very dangerous. "Get over to the sidewalk *now* or you will get killed."

She went, but reluctantly, walking in front of his Jeep and taking a last look through the vehicle window. Baryshnikov waited until she had made it to the sidewalk, and that was when he caught sight of Greet Vinckier again, her tearstained cheeks glistening under the streetlamp's light. She was oblivious to the scene that had preceded her arrival and did not realize he was there. Now it was his turn to become transfixed.

"Poor girl. Poor girl. Why so sad?" He looked as if he expected to be judged for her sorrow. "I can't help her now," he said. "Nothing I could say can help her tonight. Tomorrow will be better. Poor girl."

And so the scene ended. Yet it was worth noting, if only to point out that Mikhail Baryshnikov, who has caused a few tears to fall in his day, cannot bear to see a woman cry. It immobilized him that night. It immobilizes him when a principal dancer cries as he tries to tell her he doesn't want her in a certain role she has set her heart on. It immobilized him fourteen years before when his first love in the West subsided in floods of tears as she suddenly realized exclusivity was not to be hers. He is beside himself if his seven-year-old daughter cries. Old-fashioned as it may be, Baryshnikov will probably continue to be immobilized by women's tears right up to his grave.

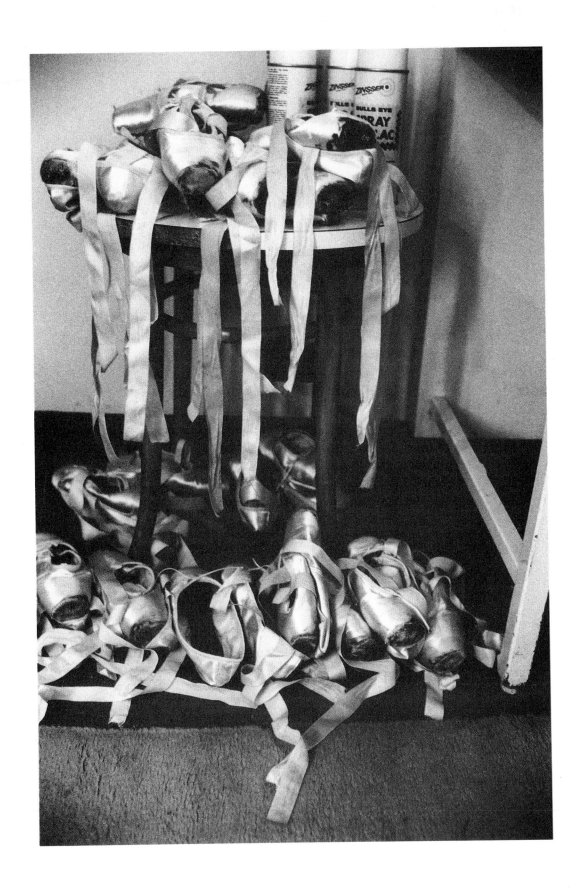

POINTE SHOES

DEATH BE NOT PROUD

*F*our months after she left Bari, Italy, Nora Kaye died of cancer at the age of sixty-seven. She had been a founding member of the old Ballet Theatre in 1939, its most famous dramatic dancer, and a former associate artistic director. Baryshnikov was told about her death while he was in the midst of company performances in San Francisco. Even though he had known her end was imminent, it came as a shock. Charles France, who was as close to her as anyone in the company, parceled his grief and carried on. Those who knew him, however, were aware that a part of him had died with Kaye. Others just as close, like Associate Director John Taras and Kaye's goddaughter, ballerina Leslie Browne, were equally saddened by her death. Kaye carried within her the soul of the old Ballet Theatre, and because she had also identified herself with the new American Ballet Theatre, Baryshnikov could think of no more appropriate honor than to dedicate the company's New York season at the Metropolitan Opera House to her memory. It was several months away, and by the time it arrived, grief would have sufficiently abated to turn the occasion into a celebration of the life of Nora Kaye. Anyway, that was the reasoning at the time. The day before the Met season was launched, however, choreographer Antony Tudor, another founding member, died in New York City at the age of seventy-nine in the midst of a revival within the company of some of his best-known works. In between these two departures, the most famous American popular dancer ever—Fred Astaire—also died. Not surprisingly, then, death was palpably in the air around ABT. The combination of these historic deaths caused many dance writers in America, and not a few traditional fans of ABT, to pause and consider not only the record of these great figures, but also the contrasts between the old Ballet Theatre they were so identified with and the newly emerging ABT being fashioned by Mikhail Baryshnikov.

*   *   *

In the beginning there was Lucia Chase and her longtime associate Richard Pleasant, both from the disintegrating patchwork quilt company created by the Russian choreographer Mikhail Mordkin, who had set up shop in the United States several years after fleeing revolutionary Russia. Pleasant was Mordkin's general manager in 1939, and Miss Chase was a competent but undistinguished ballerina who happened to have a sizable personal fortune. The combination of money and organizational skills led to the creation of Ballet Theatre the same year, with performances first given in 1940.

Even now, several years after her death, it seems impossible to speak of the founding artistic director of Ballet Theatre in any other way but "Miss Chase." Those who worked with her and knew her well within the company might refer to her as "Lucia," but if an outsider, through a modest slip of the tongue, ever says "Mrs. Chase" by mistake, there seem to be within the company's offices at least half a dozen people who will drop whatever they are doing and vociferously shout "*Miss* Chase" at the offender.

Miss Chase and Pleasant gathered around them a remarkable crew of dancers and choreographers for the first performance on January 11, 1940, at the Center Theatre in New York's Radio City. Ambitions were high, and even before the curtain went up, the reorganized remnants of the Mordkin Ballet boasted a company of eighty-five dancers, eleven choreographers, and a repertoire of twenty-one ballets, with six world premieres among them. Miss Chase's aim was to create a company that would be a showcase for the best ballets of the classical tradition and a forum for emerging modern American choreography. It was a noble and logical direction to head toward, and the redoubtable Miss Chase sank much of her fortune into the great endeavor. The results often failed to live up to the ambitions, and the artistic reputation of Ballet Theatre was destined for a roller-coaster ride for many decades. At the same time, not even Miss Chase's millions were able to keep the company from the brink of bankruptcy at depressingly regular intervals.

Yet, as it struggled to survive, Ballet Theatre developed an audience and a reputation. It became the favored American backdrop for dozens of world-famous dancers who would come and dazzle audiences and then—almost as quickly—depart for the next stop on the international ballet circuit. They came exclusively to Ballet Theatre because it was the only company that actually toured America, and the only one to feature the big classical warhorses. In addition, through all its turbulent years, it was a home for distinctive choreography, of which Antony Tudor's dark and psychologically brooding masterworks are the prime example, along with the buoyant, quintessentially American ballets of Agnes de Mille and Jerome Robbins. Whatever consistency of style Ballet Theatre had—and there was never very much of it, thanks to the lack of a clearly thought-out artistic and repertory policy—emerged not from the company's revival of the classics but from this new choreography. Since these works were all over the map, the only comprehensive adjective that could be applied to them is *eclectic.* The other factor, linking the years, was the policy of featuring stars everywhere and superstars whenever possible. After Baryshnikov defected in 1974, for example, there was no doubt about where his American career would begin.

Hitching your fate to passing stars, however, does not a great ballet company make. It generates a lot of publicity, but it can be bad for internal morale. The audiences, on the other hand, love it, and Ballet Theatre created an insatiable demand for the kind of glitter associated with the superstars, a legacy that remains strong today and has, ironically, troubled the tenure of Baryshnikov as artistic director. Perhaps that is only justice, for a superstar has a unique perception of the limitations of building a reputation around a passing fancy.

At the same time, of course, George Balanchine was fashioning his distinctive reforms to classical ballet with his own troupe, the New York City Ballet. The competition between these two very different companies has largely framed the definition of ballet in America—a competition reinforced in the public's mind by taking place in recent years in two neighboring theaters at New York's Lincoln Center for the Performing Arts. City Ballet, while never quite generating as broad a ballet audience as Ballet Theatre's, had not one but two world-class choreographers. Jerome Robbins, as the resident associate of Balanchine, provided City Ballet with the crucial emotional counterpoint missing in the master's own repertoire. It was particularly crucial after Balanchine's death, because the great man had bequeathed the company—apart from his priceless works—a negative legacy, simply by having been so brilliant: The lack of him has diminished the company not simply spiritually, but also in a dozen other ways, from the lack of a crucially commanding leader (Robbins has never, apparently, cared for the role) to the first feelings the company has ever experienced of artistic inadequacy. Miss Chase's legacy, in contrast, was to leave audiences feeling cheated if its members were unable to hurl huzzahs and bouquets at a big name when the final curtain came down.

Miss Chase was not oblivious to the necessity of creating her own stars. For one thing, it was cheaper. Still, as one sifts through yellowed clippings over the years, it is clear that she preferred importing them and then ridding herself of them. Homemade stars grew uppity and difficult to handle: Some stormed out—others lingered. The great American prima ballerina Cynthia Gregory is one dancer who had a great deal of difficulty with Miss Chase, and left her company three times. Gregory still maintains a somewhat ambivalent connection to ABT, although she and Baryshnikov, too, have had ferocious battles in the past. She is not his idea of a perfect ballerina; on the other hand, she is strongly identified in the public mind with the best of the old ABT. Gregory is still a favorite of audiences and critics, and she appears to have worked out a satisfactory relationship with the company that allows her to turn up, under her own terms, for several performances during the New York season.

In the home-grown category of stars, however, none shone brighter than Nora Kaye, born in New York on January 17, 1920. Her real name was Nora Koreff, the final two letters of her family name being the tip-off to her Russian ancestry. Now, there were ballerinas in her day who would have broken a leg or two to be born with a Russian surname. Such monikers were thought to be crucial in establishing a serious presence and career. Those who preferred to spare their bones simply changed their names, like Lillian Marks of London, England, who ended up as the world-famous ballerina Dame Alicia Markova. Nora Koreff, on the other hand, announced one day that an American dancer should have an American name. That would prove a typically assertive gesture by Kaye, who struggled mostly unnoticed in the fledgling Ballet Theatre for two years until Antony Tudor created his famous *Pillar of Fire* and cast her in the lead role of Hagar, the complex young woman who discovers love after she thinks she has thrown away all her chances.

The combination of Tudor's distinctive and often revolutionary movement within the traditional ballet technique, and Kaye's dramatically passionate interpretation, was an instant sensation. In a way, ballet has never been quite the same since, and Nora Kaye was only twenty-two at the time. Her active dancing career moved in and out of distinctive contemporary choreography: more Tudor, of course, as well as Jerome

Robbins, Agnes de Mille, and Kenneth MacMillan. In all these works, her reputation for distinctive interpretation comes down through the years as gilt-edged. In Britain, where her Giselle was regarded as one of the most distinguished of her time, she had a devoted following and was thought to be the very spirit of American dance. Her death was recorded with the sort of major obituary in *The Times* of London that is usually reserved for important national leaders.

Exuberant and warmhearted right to her dying days, Kaye was an extraordinary contrast to Antony Tudor, with whom she worked so closely for so long. Though he was widely acknowledged after his death as one of the foremost choreographers of the century, his reputation was based on a surprisingly short list of works. Most of them, however, dealt with themes unheard of in the ballet world during the years of their creation: sex, for a start, then murder, satire, and mental disorder. As *The New York Times* reported after his death:

> Tudor's advent upon the international ballet scene in the 1940s created a shock. Both his choreographic style and his psychological themes were still considered alien to the formal traditions behind classical ballet. . . . He was a genuine innovator who taught dancers and audiences to see ballet from a totally new perspective. He changed the face of ballet by his insistence that the classical dance idiom could reveal hidden desires and emotions, passions that spectators might recognize or deny in themselves.

Tudor—who also had a different name at birth, William Cook—was born in London, England, on April 4, 1908, into a lower-middle-class life. At the age of sixteen he was a delivery boy at the city's sprawling Smithfield Market. He remained there for six years, rising eventually to the lofty position of clerk. He had developed a passion for the theater and dance at an early age, thanks to regular outings to see traditional English pantomimes and touring ballet troupes—notably Diaghilev's Ballets Russes. All the time he labored at Smithfield, he spent his nights studying dance and eventually fell under the spell of Marie Rambert (born Cyvia Rambam in Warsaw) and Ninette de Valois (born Edris Stannus in Ireland). It was Rambert who managed to free Tudor from his labors at Smithfield Market and got him a modest job at her newly formed Ballet Club. He was encouraged in his choreography and began establishing a reputation.

Along with his lifetime friend and associate Hugh Laing, Tudor moved to the United States in 1940 at the invitation of Agnes de Mille to take part in the launching of Ballet Theatre. Although he would later try his hand at Broadway musicals and choreographed for a number of other companies, his life essentially revolved from then on around Ballet Theatre. At the very end, he held the title of choreographer emeritus at ABT and was busy rehearsing the revival of the ballet that made Nora Kaye so famous, *Pillar of Fire.*

Tudor's death on the very eve of the New York premiere of *The Sleeping Beauty* hit the company hard. He had been in the studios rehearsing *Pillar of Fire* only a few days previously. The official and assimilated grief earmarked for the season was all being directed toward Nora Kaye, and apart from anything else, the Tudor death came so suddenly.

The season was crucially important to Mikhail Baryshnikov and the reputation of ABT. Despite its onerous touring schedule, the exposure ABT gets in New York is what determines its reputation. An enormous repertoire was being deployed: In addition to *The Sleeping Beauty* there were full-scale productions of *Giselle, Don Quixote, La Sylphide, La Bayadère,* three Tudor ballets—*Dark Elegies, Pillar of Fire,* and *The Leaves Are Fading,* Clark Tippet's *Enough Said,* and Harald Lander's *Études.* Baryshnikov and the artistic staff had chosen everything carefully with an eye to maximum impact on critics and audiences. He didn't want to be accused of pushing the classics at the expense of new ballets, yet at the same time he wanted to show everyone the range of styles his young company could encompass—from Petipa to Paul Taylor. The direction in which he had been taking ABT had been under critical fire, and this was the season when he was going to prove the worth of creating an ensemble of young dancers who would so dazzle audiences they would forget they ever lusted after his or any other superstar's body onstage. Out of it all, he hoped, would emerge a recognition that he had begun something that had always eluded Miss Chase and her associates: a distinctive style, melded to the classical tradition and formed from American energy and excitement. It would be a style that could distinctively cope with a classic as legendary as *The Sleeping Beauty,* modern masterpieces like the Tudor work, and the very latest in innovative choreography. Some people had already accused him of selecting ballerinas who all seemed on the verge of anorexia and men whose psychological profiles could provide a medical textbook on neuroses. There is not much substance to this. It is true he likes his ballerinas trim and compact, but there are plenty of exceptions in his company. And if there are some neurotic males dancing at ABT, so are there at every company. There are even dancers whose neuroses have made them stars. Despite the brickbats, Baryshnikov has always had a concept of a company look and a company style, and this was the first season in which both these elements had come together sufficiently to build a daunting season around.

Instead of being able to stake out the high ground of his art, however, the artistic director of American Ballet Theatre was being stalked by death and injuries. As if the Tudor tragedy weren't enough, a favored ballerina—the one he planned to launch in a big way to prove that real stars emerge from a confident company with a distinctive style—was injured and had to be benched for the duration of the Met season. Instead of a gala opening, Baryshnikov was faced with a seeming debacle. Instead of seeing the curtain joyously raised on the sumptuous sets of *The Sleeping Beauty*, he was being asked to go out first and announce Tudor's death at the beginning of a season already clouded by the Kaye death and the operation for throat cancer on Sir Kenneth MacMillan, choreographer of the opening ballet.

Somehow, a number of apparently unconnected events and preoccupations in Baryshnikov's life came together that opening day in New York: the deaths of Kaye and Tudor; his growing sense of grief at the AIDS epidemic, which had robbed him of several close friends and associates; the ballerina's mishap; a critical pounding for his normally well-regarded *Nutcracker* in Los Angeles; his realization that his own dancing days were nearly over. These things were welling up inside him, and then he was told it was his duty to act as chief mourner at the Met. And he balked. He said he wouldn't do it, and that was that. Someone else could go out and pay tribute to Tudor. Some people at ABT thought he was acting from pure pique, the bad temper of a spoiled brat who was being forced to remember that there was a world beyond the one he knew, a history beyond the one he was so single-mindedly trying to create.

The crisis was evident all over Susan Jones's face in the temporary office set aside at the Met for ABT's artistic staff. The company's normally even-natured régisseur, Jones was in a flying rage and shouting at Florence Pettan.

"Well," said Jones, "if he won't go out and do this, would you explain to me who will? He is the only one who can do it right. I mean, honest to God, what is it with that man?"

Pettan agreed with Jones and so did Charles France. They had all worked with Tudor, and although they had no problems with the new artistic direction, and were in fact totally caught up in it, their careers nevertheless encompassed some of the older era and traditional lore of Ballet Theatre. It was inexplicable to them that Baryshnikov would shirk his responsibility to pay proper tribute to one of the foremost figures in ABT history.

The depth of feeling all around him was not very effectively relayed to Baryshnikov, who was busying himself with the smallest possible details of an opening night. It was clear something was deeply wrong, though. He had that look in his eyes of a hunted animal which emerges when he is under extreme stress. It had first been seen in the West shortly after his defection in Toronto, when he made his initial appearance before the international press. After he had broken his ties with the Soviet Union, people were all over him with a hundred pieces of conflicting advice. He had the look of someone backed into a corner, who saw no exit anywhere.

"You'd better do it," advised a visiting friend who knew about the turmoil in the greenroom, "because if you don't, you're going to have insurrection within your ranks and the critics will be after you till the day you die."

"Of course I am going to do it," he said wearily. "But you know, it is a very hard thing for me to do. I can't say what I want to say, so I have to act it, and for this sort of thing I'm a lousy actor."

He stopped talking for a moment and looked up at the ceiling. He looked as if he were going to start crying, but in fact it was a moment of tension release. In his mind, the crisis was over. He pulled the friend by the elbow and said very quietly, "Tell Charles I will say something."

He didn't want to talk anymore and walked off to nowhere in particular. A dancer he didn't particularly care for came up to him, but since she had a problem and the problem was concrete and immediate, he grasped it like salvation itself. "Okay, okay. I will come and see," he said to the dancer, and off the two went, almost buoyantly. On another day, under different circumstances, he might as easily have said, "See Charles about it, darling. I'm busy right now."

In *The New York Times* of April 22, 1987, dance critic Anna Kisselgoff (born Kisselgoff, incidentally) wrote:

> The death of Antony Tudor, choreographer emeritus of American Ballet Theatre and one of its founding members, could not but affect the company's opening Monday night at the Metropolitan Opera House. Nonetheless, the show did go on—in the form of Sir Kenneth MacMillan's lavish, unusually lyrical new production of ''The Sleeping Beauty.''
>
> Before the curtain went up, Mikhail Baryshnikov, Ballet Theatre's artistic director, stepped out to ask the gala audience to observe a minute of silence for Tudor, who died Sunday night. ''Tonight we want to honor his memory,'' Mr. Baryshnikov, in a husky voice, said of the English-born choreographer who had served as the troupe's associate director several times since 1940. ''His whole life was dancing, and he was truly loved by this company. We remember him with great affection and gratitude.''
>
> Despite the eloquence of Mr. Baryshnikov's words, it goes without saying that such events cast a pall. And it goes without saying that Ballet Theatre's dancers . . . did splendidly under the circumstances.

What the journalists and his own colleagues did not understand was that Baryshnikov simply did not know what to do with his grief, for it had got entirely caught up in the darker side of his life. Baryshnikov can be fairly accused of consciously or unconsciously fostering within himself a cult of loneliness, but the fact remains that loneliness is usually depressing. When he emerged through the curtains of the Met stage, with virtually the entire ballet company just a few feet behind him and the whole vast amphitheater filled to capacity before him, he felt as alone as he had ever been, except perhaps for the day his mother waved goodbye for the last time in the train station at Riga.

LAUREN PERRY

BALLERINAS

*P*erhaps Edgar Degas is the person to blame, and maybe Gelsey Kirkland's bitter book of recrimination and self-pity was the necessary antidote. Somewhere, though, between the hauntingly beautiful images of ballerinas created by the nineteenth-century Parisian painter, and the corrosive nightmare sketched by a twentieth-century American soubrette searching for an identity crisis, is the real world of women dancing. Yet to travel there is no easy task. The complexity begins, obviously, with the nature of gender itself, but it gets no less complicated as you examine female roles (onstage and off), technique, relations with dancing men, relations with artistic staff (male and female), and the aesthetic of ballet.

The art is essentially female and, in the public mind, has been dominated by female practitioners for centuries, even if men were pulling most of the strings backstage, offstage, and in the ladies' chambers. It is only a relatively recent phenomenon that strong male dancers have been given a pivotal, central role in ballet. Before Diaghilev's Ballet Russes and his wonder boy, Nijinsky, dazzled Paris early in our own century, the chief role of a man onstage was as a mere *porteur,* or hoister of ballerinas. A half century later, the women's movement has taught us to see the male fantasies inherent in so many of the famous classical roles for women in ballet. They are not malicious or evil conceptions, as such, but merely products of their times—so much so that the wonder of our age may well be that Aurora and Giselle and Odette have somehow escaped sentences of capital punishment in the high court of feminist reevaluation and revisionism, so reeking are they of male dominance and female weakness.

Most signs of female independence in traditional roles are signs of disorder, and although it may amuse some male observers to ponder the Wilis in *Giselle* as an early coven of extreme feminists, the truth is that they inhabit their ghostly, unrequited underworld because male fantasies put them there. To a diminishing extent, the syndrome still exists. Some of the tinkering done to *Swan Lake* by male choreographers during the past quarter century, for example, is virtually textbook material on the contemporary confusion of the male mind. The most famous example is Erik Bruhn's controversial version of the beloved classic, which he first mounted for the National Ballet of Canada. Here women are deposited at one or the other of the two farthest stars in the female firmament: The first is reserved for virgins and saints, and that is where we find Odette and Prince Siegfried's mother; the second is for harlots and castrating bitches, which is the world of Odile and her leader, the Black Swan Queen (translated from the traditionally male role of Rothbart the magician into a dark, satanic version of the mother figure). A simplistically homosexual resolution, this interpretation nevertheless makes for strong ballet drama onstage and is symptomatic of some of the resolutions arrived at in the contemporary business of rearranging the classics.

If Mikhail Baryshnikov ever thought that he would somehow be spared the rigors of feminist reevaluation in modern America, he has certainly been disabused of the idea by now. Although audiences and most critics are prepared to see the classics in some historical perspective, it is also true that some critics in America are after Baryshnikov's hide in this matter—or, as he himself says, "on my case." During the 1986–1987 season, a Los Angeles critic delivered something of a low blow to the Russian by attacking his concept of poor Clara in *The Nutcracker* with the help of Kirkland's juicy revelations.

Baryshnikov had restaged *The Nutcracker* for ABT in 1977, and the production, which was filmed, has become something of a tradition on Christmastime television. Like most classical companies, ABT tries to get as much mileage as possible out of live *Nutcracker* performances during the same festive season because they are such proven money earners. Baryshnikov was once lauded for boldly reinterpreting the 1892 classic and for giving it a deeply serious, even psychological interpretation. He aged Clara from a somewhat noxious tot to a mature girl on the brink of young womanhood. In this light, *The Nutcracker* became a rite of passage at a particularly important and beautiful moment in a young woman's life, and this reworking of the ballet was widely hailed as a wonderful and "refreshingly heterosexual" experiment. Dream on. In the *Los Angeles Times* of December 11, 1986, the newspaper's dance critic, Lewis Segal, revealed he had been reading *Dancing on My Grave* and suddenly realized that he had solved the riddle of Baryshnikov's restaging of *The Nutcracker*. This breakthrough revelation was duly reported:

> Gesley Kirkland's controversial recent book is a work of autobiography, not dance criticism [Segal began]. Yet its revelations about Mikhail Baryshnikov's personal and professional attitudes towards women bring into focus what has always been curious, dubious or dead wrong in his choreography. . . .
>
> By now, nearly everyone familiar with *any* "Nutcracker" knows that Baryshnikov boldly revised the plot. . . . But didn't he also transform it into a fantasy of male power and manipulation? Seeing the ballet in the light of Kirkland's book suggests no less.

We can leave aside here the novelty of a critic's interpreting an interpretation of *The Nutcracker* with the aid of an interpretation of the choreographer's interpreted motives. The point remains that women's roles in ballet are usually posited by men and are a rich source of speculation. Baryshnikov's own views and responses to women are also fair game for speculation, except for one point: He does actually like women. He likes older women and he likes younger women, although the ones in between—the ones around his own age—do seem to get shortchanged sometimes. If he is not the friend of the neighborhood feminists, neither is he an enemy to feminine ambition and assertiveness. He is gender-egalitarian in most of his moods: When he turns away from the world in despair, he doesn't differentiate between the sexes; when he's happy, everyone is invited to partake.

In the company it is true that Baryshnikov seems nominally more at ease working with the men than with the women, but the relationship to both is complex. He shares Balanchine's view that the symbol of ballet is the ballerina, and that while strong male dancing is essential and a brilliant male dancer is a treasure, the luminous and sensuous beauty of a great company comes from its women. He works them hard. Principal dancer Alessandra Ferri says "very, very hard." The life of a ballerina is cruel enough. Seen from in front of the stage, that life appears—to men, anyway—to alternate between the alluring and the ephemeral: the one quality designed to arouse; the other, to captivate. Seen from the wings— the chief vantage point for dispelling all mystery—that same life seems one of sheer physical misery relieved only by the euphoria of performance. Most people who have never been backstage would be shocked to see Aurora or Odile fly into the wings, her smile fixed serenely on her face, only to bend over in agony, grab her sides, and gasp desperately for air. Physical agony is a normal thing backstage and arouses the awe and pity only of outsiders unused to its sight, but there are occasionally some exceptionally affecting sights. One night when principal ballerina Martine van Hamel was dancing Aurora in *The Sleeping Beauty* opposite soloist Robert Hill in the prince's role, she was clearly in some special anguish. Without a word's being spoken, Hill rushed to her side even as she was gasping for air, got down on his knees, and began vigorously massaging the calves of her legs. To untie a knotted muscle? To keep her legs warm before she was able to put on some warmers? Simply to show that he was there and cared? Who knows? The need had been signaled silently and the prince was being . . . a prince.

Van Hamel provides her own classic study of a ballerina's life. Although she was only forty-one during the 1986–1987 season, she was the oldest dancer in the company, and this was the source of much of her current dilemma with the ABT artistic staff. If the critics were on Baryshnikov's case that season, and they were, it was also apparent that Baryshnikov was on Van Hamel's case. But then, according to the lady herself, there has always been someone, somewhere, making life difficult for her. The art of survival was to push on through whatever crisis emerged in her professional life, looking always to the goals she herself had mapped out. Martine van Hamel has considerable evidence to support the charge that artistic directors have always been trying to mess up her life. The success of her career, however, establishes that she also developed a steely resolve that has stood her in remarkably good stead throughout all the turmoil.

Born in Brussels into a Dutch diplomatic family, when, in the midsixties, her father found himself posted to Toronto, Van Hamel was sent to the prestigious National Ballet School there. The founder and still-reigning principal of this estimable establishment is a redoubtable woman named Betty Oliphant, who is something of a legend in the ballet world. With few traditions to build on and initially little support, Oliphant set out to create what is widely regarded as one of the top five or six ballet academies in the world. The British-born teacher knew from the beginning that she would have to offer a comprehensive education in all areas, not just ballet, if she was going to attract the kind of children she wanted. Parents were beginning to catch on to the less attractive side of a life in professional ballet, and the principal of the National Ballet School was always able to pull out her ace by justly claiming that children would receive the best all-around education in the country if they were accepted at her establishment.

According to Van Hamel, her troubles with strong-minded directors began here, almost on the first day she was enrolled at the National Ballet School. Oliphant was said to be reluctant to take her on because her father was a diplomat and would inevitably be reposted, canceling any benefit the school might give from its intensive, specialized training.

"I was tall as well," Van Hamel said, "and it was made very clear to me that this was a big problem—my big problem."

Whatever the doubts, and again this is part of the Van Hamel pattern, she made it into and through the school. Her next hurdle was as a young professional dancer with the National Ballet of Canada itself, still run by its own formidable founder, Celia Franca.

"There were certainly problems with Celia. I feel that while she did recognize my talents, she was very slow to give me roles. I remember vividly when I was finally allowed to dance the lead in *La Sylphide*. Celia made a point of telling me that I was quite unsuited for the part, but that I had been given it because they were desperate."

Another familiar pattern began emerging at this time, because audiences and critics took to Van Hamel's tall and angular good looks. She had been very well schooled and was an apt student, compensating for her tallness by a crisp, clean line of technique that registered in a straightforward way upon the people watching her. Good notices, however, do not always endear a dancer to artistic directors. In time, they can even be a major source of irritation. She could not be ignored, though. In 1966, Van Hamel had entered the prestigious international ballet competition in Varna, where she won a gold medal and became the toast of Canada—the year Baryshnikov was the male gold medalist.

The hardest time Van Hamel was ever to experience, however, was after she joined American Ballet Theatre and started crashing headfirst into Miss Chase. In 1974, Miss Chase was interviewed for an article on Van Hamel.

"We're very happy to have Martine," Miss Chase told the hometown critic, in her precisely clipped voice. "We think she's quite good . . .

[pause] . . . and I'm sure we can help her with some of her problems."

Problems? What problems?

Miss Chase smiled tightly, looked at her prim little watch, noted that she had a meeting she was already late for, and, with an afterglance as she walked away, said, "Oh, nothing serious, really, or we wouldn't have had her here. It's a question of style."

Van Hamel winced ruefully when she was reminded of this anecdote. "She never liked my kind of dancer. That's about all that can be said about it. I've always had this problem and I have always had to beg for roles. Every time. I'm still begging for roles. Somehow, somewhere along the line I keep thinking it has got to stop. I always get good reviews and normally I am very even-tempered. Now I'm being hit by this age business and it is terribly unfair. . . . I'll tell you one thing that is completely true. I have only survived in Ballet Theatre by ignoring the politics. Everything I have got, I fought for."

This age business! She didn't know the half of it. Back in the artistic staff office, whether it was at the company studios on Broadway or at the Met or at one of the dozen other temporary places the staff set up on tour, Martine van Hamel and "this age business" would crop up in one form or another.

"I have tried to explain to her that she should perhaps no longer dance Kitri in *Don Q[uixote]*," Baryshnikov said one day with genuine frustration. "I wish we could have a more realistic approach to the problem. I am no longer suited to some roles and I feel Martine is no longer suited to some others. It happens. It's simple. That's life. Why does it have to be so complicated?"

And yet, to thousands of people, Martine van Hamel is still their idea of Kitri. She is also their idea of Giselle or the Sylph or Swanilda in *Coppelia.* Many of them fell in love with her on the stage a long time ago, and in the ballet world only rats desert the ballerinas who presided over the mysteries of their initiation rites. During this difficult season for Martine van Hamel, she glided through the fervently unfriendly atmosphere with unbounded grace and nobility. In the twilight of her active dancing career, she had worked out all the frustrations that daily attended her and had entered into a pure world in which dancing alone resolved the pain and grief of the past and of an inevitable future, which had yet again been postponed for another season. Abandoned to second-night roles and the uncaring gaze of her masters, she held court with her own sense of destiny as a dancer and with the audiences that have always warmed to her.

That said, it is also true that the female members of American Ballet Theatre who surrounded her looked very different. They were shorter, skinnier, and more skittish than Van Hamel, and at times the contrast was stark. They were all Baryshnikov ballerinas, chosen and trained for the new style the Russian was imposing. "Chickens," as Van Hamel would call them: scrawny, near-emaciated chickens. That assessment did not endear her to the artistic director. There have been scenes. There have been harsh words and even tears. The casting gets more pointedly rude. There is plenty of talk of "only one more season." Although Van Hamel acknowledges that Baryshnikov has been the fairest of all the artistic directors she has had to deal with, it doesn't come across as a ringing endorsement. Although Baryshnikov will acknowledge, when he's of a mind, that she is a thorough professional, "a dancer's dancer," and still does some things remarkably well, it comes only as a concession. He is on her case, and she doesn't bend willingly, if at all. "She's one damn tough cookie, I'll tell you that," he said.

While the life of a famous principal ballerina in the company is full of such complications, it would be a mistake to think that deep down in the corps de ballet, things are easier. The swift career in ABT of nineteen-year-old Lora Smith forms the natural antipode to Van Hamel's drifting swan song. It is possibly a less cruel tale than its isolation in this account suggests, but the facts remain. Lora Smith auditioned for ABT in September 1986 after six years of increasingly intensive ballet school training, where the pressure for success can be mind-numbing—literally. Still, Smith can remember feeling sufficiently relaxed during the audition to suggest that she had made the jump to professionalism.

After the usual elimination of most of the dancers at her session, she got the longed-for telephone call. It was Susan Jones, the régisseur. Jones didn't waste time with pleasantries. The company liked what they saw in Smith but they weren't convinced that she was the right type or was even ready yet for the kind of commitment needed to dance full-time with ABT. Still, they would give her a chance, and the young dancer could sign up on a trial basis.

"It was a little freaky, I guess," Smith said at the end of the ensuing season. "This was my favorite company and now I was dancing with it. It seemed a bit like walking into a dream."

SUSAN JAFFE

DEANNE ALBERT, CYNTHIA BALFOUR, CYNTHIA ANDERSON,
CHERYL YEAGER, ALESSANDRA FERRI

CHRISTINE DUNHAM

S U S A N   J A F F E   A N D   L E S L I E   B R O W N E

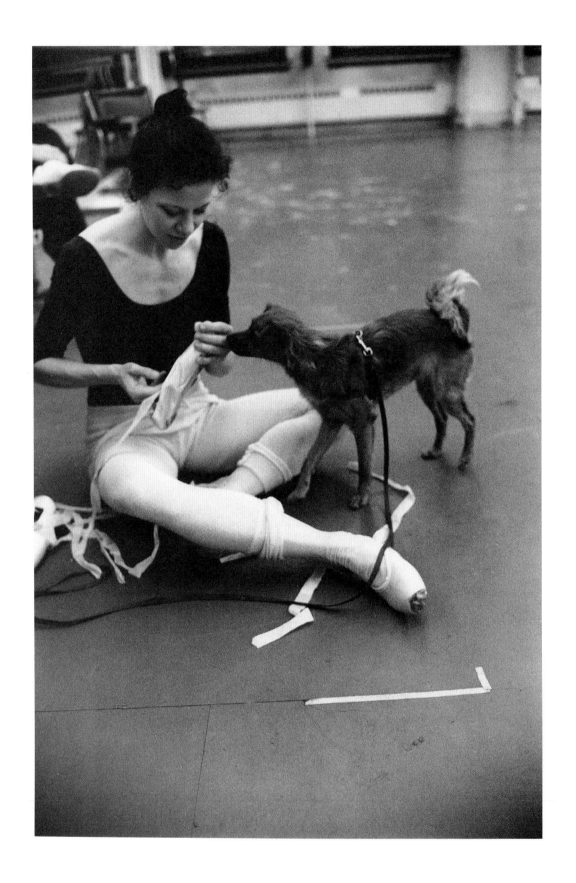

MARTINE VAN HAMEL WITH CLARK TIPPET'S DOG

AMANDA McKERROW

LYNN STANFORD PLAYING FOR CLASS

Susan Jaffe, Leslie Browne, Baryshnikov, Kathleen Moore

BARYSHNIKOV AND SUSAN JAFFE

BONNIE MOORE AND BARYSHNIKOV

LESLIE BROWNE AND BARYSHNIKOV

LESLIE BROWNE AND SUSAN JAFFE

Smith was deployed in the usual array of tiny roles it is the lot of corps dancers to perform, especially in *The Sleeping Beauty*, in which she viewed the progress of Princess Aurora as, variously, a second-act nymph, a knitting crone, and a wielder of garlands.

If it was often exhilarating just being onstage with the dancers, it was also exhausting. Lora Smith had had no conception of how tired you could get, even though she was the beneficiary of the care the company takes not to overtax the strength of new, young dancers. Often awe-struck at the physical resiliency of senior corps members who went on night after night without break, she said she frequently ended her performances in tears of sheer fatigue.

And then came the day when the artistic director called her in for "a little talk." According to Smith, Baryshnikov would not even look her in the face during the final weeks. This point has much to do with the personal chemistry of a ballet company. An artistic director does not spend a lot of time working personally with a corps member. That is the function of the ballet masters. Yet this artistic director is an incurable flirt and is not above using some of his animal magnetism to spur a dancer on in her endeavors. Lora Smith never had much direct contact with Mikhail Baryshnikov during this season, but she had a sense that he knew she was there. In the same way, she also had a sense of foreboding when even eye contact was avoided. Finally, he addressed himself to his task and apparently did it well. He talked to her about her dancing and about some of the things he liked. But he also told her she was not ready yet for ABT and would have to go.

"I think I knew it was going to happen," she said, two weeks after being told. "Everyone was very kind and I think I was told realistic things, including the chance to try to come back to Ballet Theatre. . . . Of course I was terribly disappointed and upset. But I'm a survivor and when I got over the first shock, I realized that I would be better off getting more experience elsewhere. I think I will get back here. At least I'm going to try hard."

The voice skipped in emotion a few times as she told her story, but it was clear Lora Smith had come to terms with the departure and was busy rebuilding her sense of self-worth. In nearly any other ballet company in the United States she would have survived handily and, perhaps, even have shone. At ABT she did not quite make the grade, and that was a big event to assimilate.

*   *   *

The one who left of her own deliberate choice and didn't want to come back is a very special case, so special that the Russian fell in love with her. Lisa Rinehart joined ABT in 1976 when she was just sixteen. That same year Mikhail Baryshnikov began flirting with her. He would have kept flirting, too, according to Rinehart, if ballet mistress Elena Tchernichova hadn't told him to buzz off. "She's too young, Misha," Tchernichova told him. "Leave her alone."

And he did, more or less, for six years. At the time, though, this freckled, vivacious, and intuitively intelligent redheaded beauty thought to herself, "Well, Lisa, my girl, do you want to know a really good way to ruin your life?"

Rinehart's fixation with ballet began at the age of six. She still doesn't know exactly why, but her mind was set on becoming a ballet dancer and she never veered from that course until she *was* one. Her father is a naval engineer who now works in the Department of Commerce. Her mother, like any sensible and responsible parent, did not think a career in ballet was a terrific idea. But Rinehart balked at her mother's ideas of finishing school and getting a university degree, and pushed herself so hard in ballet that she became one of the youngest dancers ever to be accepted by Miss Chase. Her bold prettiness and titian coloring make her stand out on the stage, and all that remained for Rinehart to do was to develop a sufficiently convincing technique and style to match her strong stage presence. There was also the problem of her self-confidence. It didn't exist.

"My dad always used to say that I went through life waiting to be found out, to be exposed as a fraud. I guess it was true. I can certainly remember how embarrassed I was during my first two or three years with ABT. I was sure people in the audience were looking at me and saying, 'My God, look at her. Imagine someone like her dancing with ABT.' I was a perfect little corps dancer, complete with a terror of being out of line or step. I worked at being invisible.

"By the time I was nineteen, I thought I had discovered the solution: Just don't think about it. I thought it was as easy as that. I had a boyfriend who played football and was really into training, and he decided to take on my psyche as a project. He got me to start thinking more positively about myself and told me that the trick was to stand out in the corps rather than hiding in it. At about the time Misha took over the company, I was getting so good at self-awareness that I had become totally obsessed, so much so that I nearly turned myself into an anorexic basket case. I didn't like all this very much, particularly as I was always so exhausted, but I couldn't seem to find a way out. I would dance in *Bayadere* and my legs would feel like rope. After an entire season like this at the Met, believe me, I was a burnt-out case. That's when I had my big breakthrough."

She laughed when she said "big breakthrough" because she still finds it difficult to be the star of her own stories. The bigness of the breakthrough was clearly intended to be ironic. In her own life, though, it was big enough, because Lisa Rinehart suddenly realized how much harder she would have to push herself if she wanted to make it to the very top. Unlike Gelsey Kirkland, she realized she didn't want it that badly.

"So I said no. And then I slowed down and that all seemed great, except that I got fat and a little careless and realized that I was probably losing opportunities. Charles [France], believe it or not, was always after me to lose five pounds, because he believed in me and wanted to see me succeed. But oh how they clung to me, those five pounds, and it became a real issue."

By 1982 a compromise had been reached—France had settled for three pounds—and she was chosen with other dancers to dance at the Spoleto Festival in Italy with Baryshnikov. That was when Lisa Rinehart's life became endlessly complicated because she also started "seeing" the enigmatic Russian, and it has been a special relationship ever since. Not consistently ever since, but more consistently than with anyone else.

"After years of flirting, it finally happened, and that was, well, it was . . . nice. There were some absolutely wild moments, but I was so young and naïve I always tried to pretend I could assimilate anything. . . . It took me a little while to wake up to reality."

Reality came fairly swiftly once it was learned that the artistic director had stooped into the corps—harem, some called it—to extract his latest lover. Her career instantly became the subject of intense scrutiny and speculation within the company, which suddenly became a very small community in which to be the subject of such focused curiosity. She became a recipient of both sycophancy and jealousy. Still, she had some good friends and they stuck with her as she entered the roller-coaster ride that has been her life ever since.

"When my friends saw what this relationship was doing to me, they said I was crazy. All I could tell them was that I had no choice in the matter. It made me so angry that some people thought I slept with Misha to get roles. They don't know him very well, and I knew from the first this was a very bad move for my career. Misha was so worried about the impact of our relationship that I would say I didn't get roles I might have, had we kept apart. How many times did I have dinner with Misha and Charles [France] and Susan [Jones] when they would discuss casting and who would be good in what roles? I had to bite my tongue all the time because I always wanted to blurt out, 'Hey, remember me? Little old Lisa Rinehart. That's the sort of role I could probably do.' The dancers who understood this in the company—and there weren't many—simply thought I was a fool.

"But I was prepared to sacrifice a lot during those first years. I didn't protest very much. Then Misha went to Europe to film *White Nights* in 1984, and, you know, stories filtered back. I shut my eyes to these stories and what my life had become. Whenever I opened them, I was miserable."

Rinehart laughed a lot as she recounted her story. At moments of high drama or of pointed grief, she becomes quite self-deprecating, shaking her head in mock disbelief at the things that happened to her. She has been graced with common sense and an occasionally wicked sense of humor. These assets, more than anything else, got her through intensely difficult years.

"You know, at Ballet Theatre, Misha is the boss, and some of the things he does, or has to do, seem very cruel. I would watch them happen in a way that was less disinterested than I let on. But I also saw how wounded he could become, how misunderstanding welled up inside of him and would burst out. I feel nothing but sympathy for Gelsey, and like others in the company I watched their deteriorating relationship from the sidelines with growing astonishment. But he deserved a lot of sympathy too. This bizarre world we live in demanded so much from him, and people placed so many expectations and hopes on him, that he couldn't possibly find a small space to be simply himself—to grow up in an America he didn't really know all that well at first. He is also a loving, kind, and generous person, and that is something few people give him credit for."

After *White Nights* was finished, the ardor Baryshnikov and Rinehart felt for each other cooled, and during the ensuing two years the relationship was an on-and-off one. Rinehart began this two-year period with the firm conviction that you can't count on other people to provide happiness, but she still hadn't realized that stalking happiness is inevitably futile: Happiness is the unexpected reward that comes—perversely—to those not obsessed with seeking it.

"I thought happiness was in dancing, so I threw myself into dancing and I got myself out of ABT. I auditioned for the Netherlands Dance Theater, but the atmosphere there soon struck me as slavelike to choreography. The dancers were just these little lumps of clay. I'm afraid my experience there caused the final break in my commitment to a dancing career. Another company wasn't the solution. Dancing was the problem. I woke up one day and realized dancing wasn't enough."

So she came home with a realization that dance was like a love affair—perhaps like her own affair with Baryshnikov. "You get obsessed by dancing. There seems to be no choice. Sometimes you are miserable; sometimes you are floating in elation. But you can't leave it alone until the passion is spun out. If you are very lucky, you try not to hate it when you leave. Believe me, I'm a very American dancer. I love my freedom, and I was never able to reconcile it with the dictatorial strictures which lie at the heart of ballet."

With a new sense of resolve, Lisa Rinehart registered at New York University to explore a world that suddenly seemed very welcoming. She telephoned home to tell her mother that, at long last, she was finally acceding to her wishes and getting herself properly educated.

"My dear mother, couldn't you guess, was appalled," Rinehart said, shaking her head with the kind of affectionate mystification that suggests a loving family. " 'Lisa,' my mom said to me, 'you can't give up ballet. It's so glamorous!' Well, actually, I could, and I knew I had made the right decision. I wanted out of dance and I wanted the chance to discover more things. You know, people often say dancers are stupid. That isn't so. We are sheltered and often ignorant. This can lead to self-obsession because of the demands of the system we live under. But most of us, given half a chance, can prove that we are not stupid."

She was saying all this on the spacious veranda of Baryshnikov's house on the banks of the Hudson River. He was in the neighboring garden playing with his dog. The sun dappled the verdant lawn through a filter of stout oak boughs and graceful branches of birch trees. From that distance, he seemed like an eternal boy, consorting not with destiny or stardom but with the aimless, unconscious joy of merely being alive. His old T-shirt was frayed and ripped and he was laughing at some trick he had played on the animal. A month before, Lisa Rinehart had decided to give the relationship another try. For how long, neither of them really knew. But she looked upon his lithe and eloquent figure in a way no one else ever does these days: not in admiration or awe, not with malice or loathing, not in blatant lust, not even—at least at this particular moment—with modest longing. Instead, she surveyed him with the easeful yearning of a knowing, loving friend who understood many of those things in his life that he did not like to talk about, that he could not talk about, but which he nevertheless wanted known by someone he could trust. On that pleasant summer afternoon, with Chopin nocturnes from a tape cassette floating out over the lawn, it was under this intimately known gaze of complicated affection that Mikhail Baryshnikov basked.

The process of stardom—that mysterious business in which an audience, galvanized as one, votes with its solar plexus on the aspirations and talents of a performer—is said to be unknowable. You would have a hard time proving this thesis in ABT's artistic office. Certainly, everyone there makes the appropriate noises about "only the audiences and the critics making stars" and other benign homilies. During the 1986–1987 season, however, it had been decreed from on high that Susan Jaffe would begin her emergence as a superstar, and many of the resources of the company would be directed to that end. And why not? Susan Jaffe was not only a superb dancer, she was also widely regarded as the most beautiful ballerina in the company. This was her season. This was the pivotal moment she had been training for and struggling toward all of her academic and professional life.

Born in Washington, D.C., Jaffe started training early at local schools and was nabbed as a young teenager by the School of American Ballet in New York. In 1978, she joined American Ballet Theatre II, the company's junior troupe. Baryshnikov immediately noticed her in a performance of their *Raymonda* and, believing in her potential, gave her his vote of approval: lose weight, work hard and he would take her into the senior company in the fall. His belief in Jaffe never wavered. Once she had been accepted in the senior company, it took just over three years to make the transition from corps member to soloist to principal dancer, a rank she attained in 1983. In almost every way she was the quintessential Baryshnikov ballerina: perfectly proportioned, with a strong personality and a stage bearing that could be described as imperial, confident and vibrant in her technique, stunning in her rapport with male partners, strikingly musical. That, at least, was Baryshnikov's own view, although Jaffe took a while trying to live up to it. When she started with the company, everything seemed to be going swimmingly. She got what she considered terrific roles, including Giselle, at a very early age. Then things started to go sour. Even today she's not quite sure why, and it is not easy for her to talk about that period.

"I think the official verdict was that I lacked emotional maturity to make the jump into the leading classical roles. . . . I don't know, really. It was a difficult time, and I guess I felt I had fallen out of favor. One day there were wonderful roles; the next day there were none. I started to get a martyr complex—and I carry that off very well! At the lowest point, I had just about decided to quit."

There were two reasons she didn't. The first was that initial taste of what her career might be. The second was the attention she received from ballet mistress Elena Tchernichova, to whom Jaffe ascribes most of the success of her climb back to the top. "I felt I had let Elena down," said Jaffe, "and she never gave up hope in me. Finally, I just went to her and asked for help and she gave it to me—more than I can ever repay her. She remade me." Indeed, Baryshnikov readily acknowledges the "enormous contribution" made by Tchernichova—who was with ABT before Baryshnikov was made artistic director—to the overall strengthening of the company and particularly to the refinement of its style. Charles France says simply, "She has the magic stuff."

Tchernichova worked on every aspect of Jaffe's technique and style. The ballet mistress was the first to notice that Jaffe was somewhat asymmetrical in stature and worked out a technique to accommodate what might have been a drawback. Special attention was paid to her arms, a crucial element in establishing style in classical ballet. Jaffe said she had once used her arms "like flippers." The combination of a devoted ballet mistress and a newly determined young woman paid off. When Tchernichova unveiled her reborn ballerina, everyone—and especially Baryshnikov—was very impressed.

To capitalize on her astonishing natural and freshly formulated gifts, the company had decided to build much of the Met season around Jaffe, to launch her into orbit of stardom. This is a relatively easy task to accomplish if the product to be marketed is the right one. The process starts with casting. Jaffe would dance Aurora in the opening night performance of Sir Kenneth MacMillan's new production of *The Sleeping Beauty,* which was receiving its New York premiere—which is to say the only premiere that counted, earlier tryouts in San Francisco, Los Angeles, and Chicago being merely second-city fittings. The *Beauty* premiere was to be the first message in the scheduled ABT-Jaffe onslaught of New York. The ballerina was cast in most of the important first-night roles of the other ballets throughout the season, and if all went according to plan, there would be no holding her back. The esteem the company would automatically garner for so carefully and cleverly unveiling this home-grown star was considerable. She would become the emblem of the new ABT style and the quintessential Baryshnikov dancer. In the lead-up to the Met opening, newspapers, magazines, and local television began touting Jaffe exactly as the publicity department at ABT intended her to be touted: with full-page spreads, anticipatory gush, and breathless interviews. Everything was going according to plan.

Then disaster struck in the usual way.

"About a week before the Met opening," Jaffe said, "I felt a bit of pain in my shin, but it wasn't all that distracting so I decided to ignore it. I'm known for getting a lot of little injuries and for recovering quickly. Two days later, the pain was still there, so I went to Peter [Marshall, the company physical therapist] just to double-check. I had a very positive attitude and I was trying to be careful. Peter started feeling around and hit something. He touched a point on my ankle and I just screamed. He touched it again and I screamed again. He began mumbling something about a 'stress fracture,' but I wanted no part of his diagnosis. This was the most important season in my life and nothing was going to happen to mar it.

"Misha learned that something was up and started fretting terribly, so I went quickly to get a bone scan at the hospital, convinced Peter had made a mistake. I was told that it really was a serious stress fracture above the left ankle."

In the moments after that diagnosis, she kept going over all the years of her training, her early apprenticeship, her struggle through the ranks of ABT. "It was all for this exact moment I had been working . . . longing . . . waiting. . . ." After the news from the hospital sank in, she broke down and started crying uncontrollably. When the full realization hit her, she was fortunate to be in a taxicab whose driver was sympathetic and conscientious. Her natural resiliency, for which she is also known, came into play, and she claims that within twenty minutes she had accepted that her "exact moment" would have to be postponed for a season. Walking into the company's therapy clinic, she found Marshall and Baryshnikov waiting in some trepidation.

"Misha couldn't believe it at first," she said. "He couldn't accept the timing because it seemed so specifically perverse, but he, too, soon rallied and was a great source of strength to me. I told him I thought I could at least dance the opening night if I took enough painkillers, but he urged me not to. I wasn't being stupid. I had checked with my doctor and he said I could do it, as long as I didn't try any more performances. Misha said he wanted reports from other doctors before he would approve the decision."

The consensus from the medical advisers was that the fracture would not become appreciably worse with just one performance, and so the appropriate painkillers were prescribed and administered.

"I got through the first act with relatively little pain, although I was certainly floating around the place on pure adrenaline. Adrenaline is its own wonderful painkiller. It was a lot of fun. By the end of the second act, however, the pain had become substantial, and as I prepared for the third act, I began wondering if I was in the process of destroying anything left in my career."

She got through the performance, but afterward hung up her slippers for two long, contemplative months. What sustained her the most, she said, was the careful attention of her favorite ballet mistress, Elena Tchernichova.

"Elena knows me so well. She went right into the middle of my dilemma and started building up my confidence. I owe her so much, and not just for sustaining me during these difficult days. She is the person who showed me the way to get beyond technique in a performance. That is the sort of gift you remember with deep gratitude all your life."

In the wake of Susan Jaffe's injury, the company was left with a staggering problem—recasting all her roles, a process that had something of a domino effect on overall casting and even the choice of repertoire, all at the last possible moment. In the end, the Jaffe catastrophe turned out to be a vindication for the Baryshnikov system, because the company managed to assimilate the loss of this important ballerina without undue detriment to its image, and—more important—was seen to triumph by audiences and critics. It was pointed out more than once that a truly great company can take such adversity in its stride, and this was what ABT did.

There was someone else who was vindicated. She was taller and older than Jaffe and had had no publicity buildup that season at all. Still, she moved quickly from the back ranks of principal roles to a starring position. She had no injuries worth talking about. The critics, as usual, loved her, and even Mikhail Baryshnikov pronounced his grudging admiration of her fortitude and his gratitude for her help. For Martine van Hamel, it was a very good season.

CHARLES FRANCE

F-R-A-N-C-E,
LIKE THE COUNTRY

*H*e may be only the assistant to the
artistic director, which is the unadorned truth, yet this title reveals so little
as to be meaningless. No one in American Ballet Theatre presents so
many different facets of a single personality to so many people as does the
quasi-mythic and unavoidable Charles France. Virtually any adjective
hurled in his expansive direction fits and sticks: autocratic, baleful, critical, dimpled, evasive, feisty, generous, helpful, ingenious, jaded, knowing,
lucid, manic, noble, orotund, profound, quixotic, rumormongering, sala-
cious, threatening, unyielding, vindictive, witty, xerophilous, yearning,
and especially zealous when it comes to protecting the rights and perquisites of Mikhail Nikolaievich Baryshnikov.

He is a man about whom there would seem to be no equitable
opinion. No one ever shrugs his shoulders in indifference toward Charles
France. His name, once mentioned either to a group or to individuals,
results in arching conversations which might emphasize his pivotal role at
ABT, or then again might just as easily focus on the sinister, marauding
influence he is said to wield over Baryshnikov. Both inside and outside
the company, he is the outsize lightning rod attracting any bad weather
ricocheting around the atmosphere. One thing is certain in these conversations: When things go badly for Baryshnikov or the company, Charles
France is usually to blame; when they go well, it's Charles Who?

To see the extraordinary France in action is not necessarily helpful in
trying to come to terms with him. In action—or, rather, unleashed—he is
awesome to behold, a force Nature herself would be loath to redirect. At
ABT, depending on the moment you catch him when he is on the go, and
he is always on the go, he might be found at the very heart of darkness,
plotting terrible strategems against real and imagined enemies. Then again,
he might just as easily be discovered as an angelic panjandrum in the

realm of pure light, where his impeccable artistic taste and sense of due proportion have once again resolved a mishmash of half-baked schemes and ideas that threaten to destroy an ill-conceived season. He is that rarest of persons in the performing arts: a man of vision and practical common sense.

More than any other person in the company, except Baryshnikov himself, Charles France *is* the pivotal figure, and this is the source of much of the controversy surrounding him. For many people outside the company, and even a number inside, Charles France is considered the real artistic director and Baryshnikov merely his puppet. The truth is very different, but it is easy to see why the error is made. To begin with, France has a way with words, and his master tends to guard his tongue—at least in public.

Baryshnikov's hotel suite in Bari, Italy, where a representative of *Paris Vogue* came calling during the autumn of 1986, was the setting for a quintessential demonstration of one aspect of the France style and of the symbiotic relationship he and Baryshnikov have forged over the past decade. *Paris Vogue* was handing over its high-profile end-of-year edition to Baryshnikov in a celebratory extravaganza, the profits of which were to go to AIDS research. It wasn't just a special edition on the Russian. He was, in effect, asked to be the editor, choosing the writers and pictures, and mapping out special features, which included a wild and campy retelling of *Swan Lake* that would eventually become a separate book, *The Swan Prince*, also designed to raise funds for AIDS research.

To Baryshnikov the project offered the signal opportunity to show his bona fides as a serious and thinking artist, as well as a playful humorist. He lined up some of his favorite people to write for *Paris Vogue*, including the Nobel laureate Joseph Brodsky, the eminent *New Yorker* magazine dance critic Arlene Croce, film directors Milos Forman and Roman Polanski, and the essayist Susan Sontag.

And then, one sticky September evening, the *Paris Vogue* man came from France to Italy with the final layout and editing changes, along with his wife of only two weeks. Before their meeting took place, Charles France had carefully gone over the editing job with Baryshnikov, and the two of them were beside themselves with rage. It wasn't just the photographs which had been so sloppily laid out, although that was a major irritant. *Paris Vogue*, not fully appreciating the world of dance in New York, had inexpertly eradicated large parts of key writers' meticulously crafted prose and then referred to Arlene Croce, the doyenne of ballet critics, in a typically condescending Parisian manner. In her piece, "Le Mystère Baryshnikov," Croce had written one of the most beautiful tributes ever paid to a dancer: "What a Baryshnikov performance means we cannot say. It is as necessary and unremarkable as clean air, clean water, and light." This phrase had mysteriously disappeared.

As the full import of this injudicious editing sank in, the language became very blue in Suite 1011. "My God, my God!" exclaimed Baryshnikov. "Do they not know who these people are? How do they think I will agree to this ****ing cr**-sh**? I will kill this man when he comes. I will take my hands around his ****ing neck and . . ." This conversation continued in much the same vein until the buzzer rang at the door. Quick as a snap, Charles France looked at Baryshnikov in dead earnest. "Misha," he said, "let me be the heavy this time. Okay?"

"Okay, okay," snarled Baryshnikov. He was about to pontificate on what the magazine had done to Brodsky when the buzzer intervened again.

The Frenchman and his young wife walked into the room, full of confidence as well as that instant camaraderie that very famous people must put up with as the price of their celebrity or notoriety. Baryshnikov was still trying to emerge from his sulk and could barely manage a vinegary smile before he retreated to a corner of the room and wrapped his arms around himself. No drinks were offered. Cigarettes were not encouraged. The young wife, who had undoubtedly been brought along to watch her man deal efficiently with the great Baryshnikov, was instantly ignored. The resourceful and experienced Lisa Rinehart had already retreated to the adjoining bedroom when she figured out what was up. "I think I'll leave this scene, thank you very much," she said with a tight, knowing smile. "I've seen the dynamic duo work people over before. It's not such a pleasant sight. You can mop up the blood if you want to. I'm going to read my book."

Blood?

Guts, spleen, sinews, bone marrow, and heaven knows what else glistened metaphorically on the thinning shag carpet before a half hour was up. Charles France on the warpath is more powerful than a speeding locomotive and able to leap over ordinary rules of civility in a single bound. His fluent, richly decorative French has a distinct nasal twang not dissimilar to what Bette Davis came up with during the more breathless moments of *Hush, Hush, Sweet Charlotte*. He laid out the pages from *Paris Vogue* on the floor and coffee table as a professor of anatomy might do the butchered relics of a student project.

"Je vous assure, Monsieur, que M. Baryshnikov insiste absolument . . ."

"I promise you, sir," said France, "that Mr. Baryshnikov is going to insist that you get this project right or you can forget the whole thing. What you have done is a scandal, an outrage. What on earth were you thinking when you . . . ?"

France, when he is raging in whatever language—and he can throw around at least four—deploys a slightly lisping "s" like a cat-o'-nine-tails. The words lacerate all attempts at defense or riposte. The glasses fall down a little on his nose and he pushes them back in a menacing gesture that somehow suggests he is getting ready to devour his victim. The Frenchman's jaw sagged under the relentless assault. He kept trying to interject explanations, or alternatives, or apologies, or anything that would turn off the spigot on Charles France's invective, all to no avail. The assistant to the artistic director of ABT seemed a man possessed, and it was a spectacular performance. As it reached its height, the very point where it seemed this enormous mass of humanity might actually propel himself off the ground on a trajectory of rage, the silent, brooding figure in the corner smiled sweetly and spoke in such a soft, assuaging voice that everyone turned to him in arrested amazement. Everyone except Charles France, of course, but then he knew how the script went. He was the "bad cop," and it was time now for the "good cop" to take over.

"Charles, Charles, that's enough," said Mikhail Baryshnikov, who might well have been inspired by a vision of Saint Francis of Assisi. "Don't forget this poor man has come all the way from Paris and we must find a calm way out of these problems. I'm sure he wants to get everything correct, just as we do. We should forget these angry words and see what we can do. Don't you agree, Monsieur . . . Monsieur . . . ?"

Maybe he had forgotten the name, maybe he hadn't. Whatever the case, Monsieur lunged at the proferred olive branch with equal measures of gratitude and sycophancy. Within minutes, Croce had been restored, Brodsky healed, better picture displays suggested. The *Paris Vogue* man had traveled from self-parody to the realm of undiluted pathos. "Yes, yes, but of course," he kept saying. "Everything will be just as you want. . . ."

France narrowed his eyes. "That's what we were told the last time, Monsieur, and we have seen the disastrous results. How do you plan to make sure we see the final product before it is too late to correct another catastrophe?"

The logistics were worked out, the scattered papers gathered up, and the Frenchman backed out of the room, almost forgetting his bride of two weeks. It had been a bum rap in many ways for the poor man. He wasn't responsible for the editing, but he was the messenger for *Paris Vogue* and had to take home all the messages, which included the news that Charles France himself would be coming to Paris to help supervise and approve the final edition.

When the door clicked shut, the two actors looked at each other in mutual admiration until Lisa Rinehart came in from the bedroom and broke the moment of silent revelry.

"Everyone have a nice time?" she asked briskly.

To do the master's bidding is not the most thankful job in the world. The Number Two position in any organization—whether it is the Politburo, the White House, or just the Neighborhood Watch Committee—rarely offers more than two approaches: plotting against or quietly enduring Number One. Charles France has found a third alternative, one usually reserved for those who serve monarchs, popes, or dictators: He has abdicated all his own obvious self-interests and sworn an oath of constancy and fealty to Mikhail Baryshnikov that seems vaguely feudal in its fervor. Whatever advances the cause and interests of the Russian also advances his own cause and interests; whatever detracts, whatever denigrates, demeans, or in any other way undermines Baryshnikov is attacked without quarter. There are deep and complex reasons for this, some of which he is prepared to talk about with eloquent conviction; others, he merely hints at. The reaction of the beneficiary of all this focused attention, however, is unambiguous: "It's quite simple, really," Baryshnikov says. "I would not be where I am today without Charles. Period. No more debate."

Charles France was born in Oklahoma City in 1946, the son of a prosperous attorney who had been in the judge advocate's department in the army, leaving the service with the rank of colonel. His mother was Danish-born, well-traveled, and, judging from France's continuing affection for her, a major influence during his early years, especially after his father died in 1952 when France was only six. His formative youth was spent in a succession of schools on both sides of the Atlantic as his mother moved restlessly between America, Denmark, and France. Although Charles usually did well at these various schools, he was by his own admission "a disciplinary problem" until he finally made it into a university where his natural skills as a linguist led him to the Ph.D. program in French literature at Columbia.

At the time, and it was before he took on the great bulk of weight with which he is so mightily identified today in the ballet world, he thought he fancied an academic life. To this end, France managed to complete all the technical requirements for a doctorate at Columbia University before abandoning the whole enterprise and embracing what he finally recognized was the only uncomplicated love of his life: ballet.

"My mother sent me to ballet school at the age of seven in Oklahoma City," he said. "What can I say? I liked it. I had a wonderful teacher from the Ballets Russes de Monte Carlo, and it was fun. God, you should see some of the fabulous photos of me in recital. You have to see them. I was once adorable, you know. We went to ballet performances a lot too. I was taken by my mother and her set, although really they preferred opera. Then, when I was nineteen and came to New York to live, I started going to the ballet regularly. I was besotted. Very, very impassioned. Every night there was something on somewhere, I went. For six years! I'm not exaggerating. I was possessed. Eventually I started doing some dance writing, especially with *The Village Voice* and *Ballet Review*. There were some wonderful interviews, too, with Eliot Feld and Danilova and . . ."

The telephone rang. It was not possible to talk to Charles France for longer than four minutes and twenty-three seconds without either the telephone ringing or France dialing. This particular call, in a hotel room in Washington, was the seventeenth that day on the same subject. France is an obsessive. This is the key to understanding his personality on a practical day-to-day basis. To anyone who knows him, it is not at all strange that he would spend the better part of an entire working day tracking down one relatively minor aspect of his responsibilities. In this case, it was an effort to get the right photographer teamed up with a specific project. The business had taken on a life of its own, because he was worried that the wrong photographer and a diverted project would be injurious to American Ballet Theatre and Mikhail Baryshnikov.

So his fingers became demons on the telephone buttons that day, and woe betide any poor soul who tried to come between Charles France and the mouthpiece. Between the fifth and sixth phone calls, that soul—in the form of a corps dancer—hesitantly entered the artistic office set up for the ABT season at the Kennedy Center in Washington. She took up a position in front of France's desk, where he proceeded to ignore her as he gave a senior executive's secretary a very hard time.

"Would you tell him Charles France, calling for Mikhail Baryshnikov, would like to speak to him as soon as possible on an extremely urgent matter. I want you to attend to this personally. What did you say your name was? I'm writing that down. . . . I told you my name. It's France. F-R-A-N-C-E. That's right, just like the country."

When he hung up the phone, still more than a dozen calls away from final victory, the ballerina cleared her throat—not aggressively, just the mildest sort of "ahem." As he picked up the phone receiver, France looked at her and glared. Indeed, he tried to glare her out of the room. But while she did look crestfallen, she did not flinch or otherwise move at all.

Two more brief phone calls found him closer to the kill and his mood was easing up. Yet he was on a roll and didn't want to stop. The last phone call had opened up opportunities to new angles of strategy: For the first time that day, he was beginning to enjoy himself. He started to dial again.

"Please, Charles," blurted the dancer. She sounded like Oliver Twist asking for a second bowl of porridge at the Victorian workhouse. "I must speak to you about . . ."

France had pushed the third or fourth digit of the latest call and kept his fingers on the telephone buttons. Looking directly at the young woman, his bearded face became distorted in angry mystification. How could she still be there after he had glared her away? How could she still be there when it was perfectly clear that he was on a roll, a mission, a fix-all? How could she still be there when she knew that he knew all about her problem, including the singular fact that right now was certainly not the time to discuss it? How, in short, could she still be there?

"Go away," he said.

"But Charles, I . . ."

"I'll fix it later. Go away!"

She went away as his eyes widened in amazement that anyone could have the temerity to try to stop his work at its most crucial moment and while he was actually getting somewhere. He redialed the number and was off once again on the hunt. In a corner of his notepad, however, he jotted down the banished dancer's name. She would get her own turn at his undivided attention as soon as he could provide it, which wasn't yet.

At this epochal juncture, with the crisis of the day nudging toward a happy resolution, Charles France allowed as how it might be safe to take a short break. He made it out into a second-floor hall at the Kennedy Center, into the elevator, and out toward the stage door. With a sense of timing only Florence Pettan could have arranged, the telephone at the stage door security office rang just as France entered the final foyer.

"You're right! How did you guess?" the security officer said as he saw France come through the door. "Here he comes right now."

France was off in telephone land once again, this time for nearly ten minutes. Dancers came in and out of the stage entrance and nonchalantly said "Hi, Charles" to him as they went by. He brushed all of them aside. The older dancers smiled knowingly at each other. It was Charles obsessed. The younger dancers, the ones who didn't know him well at all, took it very personally. On a billboard beside the security desk where France was talking was a small poster:

HOLISTIC BODYWORK, it began. DEEP TISSUE MASSAGE THERAPY! CRANIOSACRAL BALANCING! EMOTIONAL RELEASE! ALIGNMENT! RELAXATION, INSPIRATION, HEALING. KUNO BACHBAUER: HOLISTIC SERVICES. CALL TODAY.

Attached to the poster were individual cards with direct telephone numbers to this center of craniosacral balancing and emotional release. Charles France did not take one.

"To regard me as some sort of Svengali in Misha's life, you know, implies that he is not capable of operating on his own. This is simply not true. It implies that our relationship is somehow secret, which is a real joke. And, if I may say so, it also ignores how conscientious I think I am in making sure Misha sees things, knows things, understands his choices, understands the consequences. That is because he has to make the decisions. He doesn't have any problem making decisions. He's very business-like, very professional. He expects and deserves equal professionalism from me and Susan Jones and Flo[rence Pettan]."

In this instance, anyway, Charles France does not protest too much. Although Baryshnikov admires him, and depends upon him more than anyone else in many areas of his professional life, he also knows that many people in the company and on the board intensely dislike him. In a way, he protects France even as France protects him. This mutual safeguarding of interests has its parameters. Although it doesn't happen often, Baryshnikov does not hesitate to pull France down a peg or two when he's of a mind. Once, in Chicago during a dress rehearsal for *The Sleeping Beauty*, France was almost beside himself; he was trying to get Baryshnikov's attention in order to slow down his stage directions so that a host of visiting news photographers could get a certain shot. Baryshnikov, mindful of union time for the stagehands and anxious to push on, simply ignored the heavy coughing nearby, and the insistent hiss. Finally, France blurted out, "Misha, can we just pause here for two minutes to give these people a chance to take their pictures?"

"*Charles!*" Baryshnikov exploded in front of everyone in the theater. "I am still giving direction."

And that was it.

France, like all Number Twos, inadvertently gives the impression that he runs the company, because he has to do so much of the master's bidding, especially the dirty work. It is France, or one of his assistants, who must relay the bad news on casting, who must tell Larry Lynn to go stuff himself, who provides a stalwart buffer between the artistic director and Charles Dillingham, who must tell the publicists and journalists and photographers and board members and society matrons who want to get close to Baryshnikov that they should buzz off, fast (or tell the very opposite to Baryshnikov, if the need is deemed important enough). The newer dancers in the company have not figured this out yet; a few of the older ones understand it implicitly. "I never mind anything Charles says," said Martine van Hamel, who has certainly been the recipient of many an unwelcome message from the top over the years. "We go back so far in this company that we know each other inside out. It's never a big deal with Charles. The traffic between us is too familiar. I tend to rely on him for his honesty."

On a rampage, he can be frightening to behold, and there are people at ABT who simply shudder at the memory of France in extremis. His language can become grotesque, and because he is such a canny student of human nature, he can rip into people with withering effect. The business he is in is mostly all high-risk stuff, and he has carved out for himself a virtually impossible job profile: factotum of a classical ballet

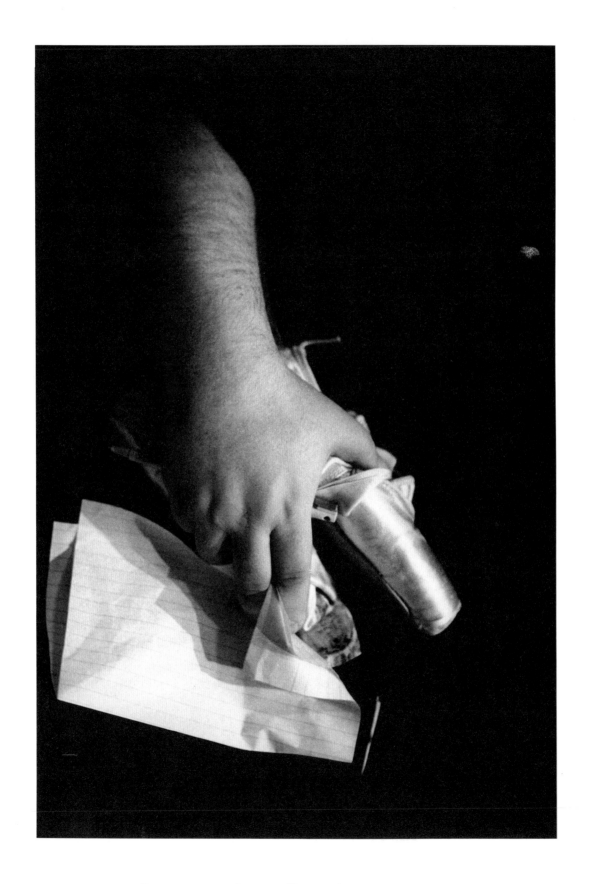

FRANCE WITH CHERYL YEAGER'S POINTE SHOES

FRANCE, JULIO BOCCA, ALESSANDRA FERRI

BARYSHNIKOV AND FRANCE LOOKING AT DESIGNS
FOR BARYSHNIKOV BODYWEAR

FRANCE AND BARYSHNIKOV REVIEWING A SCRIPT

company and chief manager of a superstar who also happens to be the artistic director. It is up to him to reconcile conflicts between his different responsibilities, and sometimes there is no room for reconciliation. It would be a lot easier for Charles France if he were as brutal as he sometimes seems to others. In fact, he can be wounded quickly and easily, and although his sense of humor is wide and usually generous, he occasionally suffers deeply from the anomalies of his job. An incident that occurred two weeks before his account of it was still festering inside him, although, with forehead furrowed, he made a major effort to tell the tale unadorned by his usual bric-a-brac of baroque wisecracks and rolling eyes.

"The mythology that gets built up in a ballet company eventually carries real weight and it can become distressing. A little while ago, we botched a casting for a ballet that was part of a package of works we planned to tape for television in Copenhagen. There was a nice trip involved for the dancers we chose, as well as major media exposure. Around here, it was very important. The casting was all done except for a woman's role in one sequence, because Misha couldn't yet decide between two girls. He said he wanted to see another performance before making up his mind. So I said fine. We would put up the casting list, which had been all agreed except for the woman's role, which was just left TBA [to be announced]. For some reason, that list didn't get put up. We seemed to be inundated in pieces of paper that day in the office. When Misha saw the performance he wanted to check out, he said, 'I want this girl to do it.' But he then went on to make an extra change in another sequence.

"God help me, we then put in the name of the wrong girl in the casting list by mistake and posted it. Now you know Misha well enough to realize that he might have forgotten his final choice if we had said nothing and just let it ride. I admit I was tempted to try that route, but in the end I knew it was wrong. I had to tell him that I had made this terrible mistake. So I told him. I told him I had loused it up, and what did he want me to do about it? 'I'm truly sorry, Charles,' he said to me, 'but I want who I chose.' Fine. Great. Since I had made the mistake, I was the one who had to tell Anna Spelman (a senior corps dancer) that she wasn't coming to Copenhagen after all."

France paused here to stretch and brood for a moment. Part of his dilemma is that he is unbelievably overworked. Everyone in the artistic office does far too much, and because this work involves hundreds of minute details, it is surprising that more mistakes are not made.

"It was not pleasant," he continued. "As you might expect, she was hysterical, I mean *hysterical*. It was a very hard thing to deal with, and I was extremely embarrassed because I really like Anna. I like her dancing; I like her looks; I like her energy. But you know how things are. And she just went at me. It wasn't Misha's decision, it was mine, she said. She knew how much Misha appreciated her. As for me, I had overruled the artistic director because I like the other girl so much better. I would have given anything not to go through that scene. It's very demoralizing to everyone involved, and profoundly uncomfortable. But Mikhail Baryshnikov is the artistic director of American Ballet Theatre, and what he wants to happen should happen. I try to bring him options and explain implications, but in this case to have done anything different from what I did would have been a lie. It bothered me very deeply that Anna Spelman had to be hurt that way, more than she or any of the other dancers will ever realize. If it had been my decision to make, it would have been Anna Spelman who would have gone to Copenhagen."

Since he looms so omnipresently in their professional lives, many of the dancers and some of the ballet staff spend a lot of time excoriating and exorcising Charles France. On a day-to-day basis, the relationship with quite a few of them is reasonably pleasant, but it needs only an incident to send the barricades up, and Charles France is transformed once again into an arch-villain. He has his spies, of course, and he is not loath to receive information, but he has developed a very keen appreciation of the difference between gossip that is irrelevant, harmless, and sometimes amusing, and poisonous myths that are positively detrimental to the company or Baryshnikov.

"I do care about what people in the company think about me wherever there is a dangerous gap between that thinking and reality. That often spells real trouble in some form or another. On a personal level, I guess I sometimes brood about the gap between the way I am seen and where my heart is. A lot of the dancers know that I spend a great deal of time thinking about them and the company. My impression is that most of them are not particularly articulate on my positive points and find it easier to express themselves on what they see as the negative ones. On most days I can live with that, although I can get outraged and incensed when I hear really twisted stories. It's human nature, I guess, but my nature is human as well."

The artistic office is not the place for quiet work when someone there gets wind of a dancer who is sounding off in public against him or her. If word comes via an article in *The New York Times* or *Dance Magazine,* the atmosphere can be wild, especially if the offending article compounds a "one-sided" view with incorrect information about the company or the artistic director, at which point France can go into a near-paralytic rage.

"It is always very difficult for me to not feel enormous frustration when people outside the company make any sort of evaluation without all the relevant information. The public and the press do not have the ability—or the desire for that matter—to understand that a ballet company is mostly minutiae and complicated psychological conundrums. There are always very dramatic and volatile and mysterious issues floating around here, and it is practically impossible to understand them from the outside. Everything always gets reduced to such a simplistic level.

"A press person will usually accept, without qualification or further checking, what someone at the age of twenty will say if he or she is disaffected with the artistic policy of the company. In fact, that dancer may be in a very poor condition, with a totally unrealistic sense of his or her capabilities. That the dancer is aggrieved is real enough, but maybe— just maybe—there is something of a story from the other side. Maybe, on the other side, there have been some terribly difficult decisions that had to be taken. Maybe—just maybe—the artistic staff were trying to consider the overall company in taking that difficult decision. And maybe—just maybe—that decision caused as much grief, or more, to the artistic staff."

Charles France does not often talk like this, and he only did so here because he had been goaded by a random sampling of backstage gossip and analysis of his role. Nevertheless, it is important in assessing such a *de profundis* to realize that there is no one in the company who has been as immersed in so many areas as this remarkable man, who seems to be balancing on a teeter-totter while simultaneously juggling a hundred plates in the air. Before coming to ABT, he worked as a dance writer and critic and knows very well how easily glib opinions rise up and find their way into the holy writ of print—although, like most former journalists, he has forgotten how quickly a bad review or a troublesome interview is forgotten by the public.

He first came to ABT as a summer employee in 1971 and for several years scrambled around doing any job the company had to offer. What he doesn't know about group ticket sales, promotional mailings, fund-raising campaigns, boutique sales, publicity releases, the myriad offstage irritations of dancers great and small, and the perils of service to artistic directors, isn't worth knowing. He has a strong, outsize personality to match his physical dimensions, so that while it has always been recognized that he may well be the most single-mindedly devoted servant to ballet ABT ever took to its bosom—and that does not exclude Miss Chase, although Florence Pettan might be the single exception—France has never inspired a lukewarm response.

In a strange way, most dealings with Charles France end up telling you more about yourself and your attitudes than they do about him. It is often the way with very strong personalities, especially very strong, controversial personalities. For his own part, the fervor of his devotion to ballet is a clear and almost holy manifestation of his longing and determination to make a commitment. And so it is that his minor acts of perceived treachery and arbitrariness, which in isolation can sometimes seem inexplicably cruel, are wholly caught up in a personal agenda marked by restless searching for a definition of excellence in the most ephemeral of the arts.

American Ballet Theatre was a sufficiently large and complicated troupe to keep him running at full steam when he was climbing its hierarchical ladder. What threw him for a titanic loop, and has kept his life in self-imposed turmoil ever since, was the first sight he ever had of the young lord of the dance. France has a very clear recollection of this pivotal moment in his life. He believed he was watching the greatest male dancer he would ever have the privilege of seeing, and that in Mikhail Baryshnikov he had found—at last—a focus for his many tangible and inchoate ambitions.

When Charles France traveled to Montreal in June 1974 to take a look at Mikhail Baryshnikov and the touring troupe he had accompanied from the Soviet Union, he was going through a difficult period at ABT. He had, by his own admission, a "bumpy relationship" with Miss Chase, who found him too independent for the company's (i.e., her own) good and far too opinionated about things she didn't want to know about. He was then working full time in the public relations office, and he loved the work. He even admired Miss Chase, in his fashion, and despite their periodic disputes, he knew that he basked in her favor because the job he held for five years as director of public relations and marketing was crucially important to ABT.

He had a smoother relationship with Oliver Smith, the other great formative figure at ABT, and was promoted to be his assistant for one year. The era surrounding the moment Baryshnikov defected coincided with the peak period of the last generation of superstars in ballet. Inside ABT there was intense friction—as sporadic outbursts of anger preserved in yellowing newspaper clippings testify. The position of the native-born American prima Cynthia Gregory always seemed to be challenged by Natalia Makarova, one way or another. Later, this would be violently echoed in the rivalry between Baryshnikov and Fernando Bujones.

Once Baryshnikov joined ABT, France immediately recognized that the company had a unique chance to be associated with an astonishing artist who could have an enormous impact on the company's artistic potential. As he observed the ferocious energy of the man, he also drew closer and closer to him personally.

"One of the things Mikhail Baryshnikov did during this period which was critical to his stardom was that he made sure everyone saw him regularly in the great classical and romantic roles, while [he took] on everything else that he could find from contemporary choreography. He put himself in front of his public three, four, five times a week in a lot of different things. This has stood him in great stead, and, in our world anyway, he was the first great star to become readily accessible to audiences. He also developed a fabulous reputation with choreographers who longed to build works around him."

France started taking the measure of the Russian almost from the first day he joined the company. He accurately gauged the intensity of his drive when Baryshnikov was actively dancing, and judged his capacity to relax and let his defenses down when his ballet slippers were off. Rather than wanting to get to know him, he studied the man closely while everyone else made assumptions or tried to force Baryshnikov into a personality of their own choice. In time, almost alone of all the people who have encountered Baryshnikov since he defected, France came to understand the man he was dealing with. There is simply no way the Russian could have survived in the company, or have been led in directions profitable to his own career, without this great, bounding slab of humanity constantly at his elbow. Taking command and embracing difficult decisions are not problems for Baryshnikov; proper—or at least appropriate—deployment of leadership and decisions, however, is a problem. In deployment, Charles France is the Marshal Ney of ballet. One of Baryshnikov's greatest and most successful breakthroughs was to recognize this specific genius, to trust it, and finally to use it. He also fussed terribly about France's weight and still nags him to take remedial action, knowing that his friend's health—and possibly his life—depends upon it. Ironically, Baryshnikov also seemed to recognize that the rotundity may somehow be tied to the exclusivity of France's devotion to him. By removing himself from so much that acts as currency in ballet—lean bodies, transparent sexuality, surface slickness—France has also made a transition into a world of pure service, devoid of sycophancy and replete with common sense.

Nowhere has this common sense been more obvious, or controversial, than in the area of what we might call the subsidiary business endeavors of a superstar. Some of Baryshnikov's strongest balletic admirers howl with rage when they see him endorsing a line of clothing, or introducing a bottle of perfume, or taking another role in a clumsy film, or grinning disingenuously in "inappropriate" popular television specials. But France has encouraged him in many of these efforts for several reasons, not the least of them financial.

"I do support him in all facets of his career, and I try to support him to the best of my capabilities. Mikhail Baryshnikov is a very great dancer and his stardom, even during these days, when he is required to slow down, is still heavily invested in his role as a dancer. Yet, for a variety of reasons, he has not been able to earn the tangible rewards of such a stardom. He does not have a whole heap of money. Partly this has been because he has danced so faithfully for so long with repertory companies, especially here at ABT during the years right after the defection. As an artist, he showed remarkable courage and vision when he joined the New York City Ballet to work with Balanchine. As an emerging superstar, of course, it was sheer madness. Those were the years he could have been amassing the money to look after the long years he must face in dancing retirement, and the money would have been easy to amass simply by traveling the international superstar circuit as a celebrated guest artist.

"I have been supportive of his association with certain commercial ventures—not all—which will give him a security and reward consistent with what we may as well call the American way of life. None of the things he has done, in my opinion, has compromised his poetic image. I guess you could say there was a Soviet alternative, complete with state pensions, but the total picture there never turned me on much. Given his talent and the efforts he has made to harness it, is it more or less honorable to endorse a line of perfume than to dance under vile conditions? Endorsing a line of ballet and exercise body wear is a logical extension of his business. I have never understood this thing about commercialism affecting artistry. He doesn't go onstage with Adidas on. When he is onstage, his artistry and standards are wholly on view, intact, true, and pure. That is how he has been able to obtain and keep his nobility.

"Of course all sorts of people are after him to do all sorts of things. If he went into some degrading and terrible film for ten million dollars, then maybe people might have the right to point a finger and shout about self-corruption. But I know him quite well, you know. He is incapable of being vulgar. In the areas where he has direct control over his own image, he has always demonstrated unerring good taste."

This was getting very close to the heart of the matter. France did not choose to talk about the one film project Baryshnikov did—*White Nights*—that France was shut out of, where his advice was not heeded or called for. The film, about a defected Russian dancer who ends up back in the Soviet Union following an emergency plane landing—was not great, but it was also not that bad. Indeed the first twenty minutes, beginning with a brilliant performance on the ballet stage and continuing through an exciting airplane crash sequence, promised a riveting popular entertainment. But then *White Nights* got bogged down in stereotypes and ever-increasing improbabilities, which shocked and dismayed many in Baryshnikov's immediate entourage, although the film was not unpopular with audiences. Still, both men stay off the subject of this film, at least when they are around each other. Their relationship is too mutually important to allow room for specific recrimination.

"I am entirely devoted to Mikhail Baryshnikov," Charles France said, with a face as serious as he ever shows. "I have a certain healthy and vicarious pleasure in his successes and get vicarious depressions during his low moments. I think that I understand him very well, although he still manages to surprise me many, many times. I'm not jaded about him. He has a refreshing mind and he is not lazy. He is a great artist and that means a great deal to me personally. I devote my life to him, and it is important to me to believe that this commitment has been made to someone who is crucial to our art. This is what has given me the emotional attachment to him and has intensified my loyalty and protectiveness.

"I don't always have the best advice for him. I'm just one person and I don't have all the answers. But I have been well educated in this business. I've had a complicated and diverse preparation for the work that I do and the service that I can offer him. I feel tied to him in endlessly intricate ways, and undoubtedly a great deal more than he would like to know about . . ."

Charles France looked out a window as he pushed his glasses up from the tip of his nose. The pause had been for only a second, but he finished the sentence in a whisper.

". . . or ever should know."

VICTOR BARBEE AND BARYSHNIKOV

DANCING MEN

American Ballet Theatre today is a company headed by a superstar who mostly disdains the services of superstars. Started by an American who tried to infuse European traditions into its performances and repertoire, ABT is now run by a Russian who glories in American values and energy. Yet in the house of ironies that Mikhail Baryshnikov has built, the most intriguing item is his relationship with the male dancers. Very few of the men dancing at ABT did not at some time or another witness the phenomenon of Baryshnikov the dancer in his prime, and with that signal act, many of them were inspired to dedicate or redirect their professional lives. More than the women dancing there—much more—the men look to Baryshnikov for continual confirmation of their careers, for practical coaching on the specifically male aspects of technique, for interpretation of roles, for praise and corrections, for any form of information that will impart to them some of his magic.

Even if he were a different sort of man than he is—more naturally spontaneous, say, or less jealous of his privacy and less wary of being used—it would be impossible to deliver on all the expectations that greet him each time he enters a ballet class or directs a rehearsal. As it is, he tries hard to deliver on some of what is expected of him, but it is never enough. The desire of many of the male dancers to be closer to him, to share a more equitable relationship, is its own barrier. Sensing this, they usually draw back and are reluctant to express their gratitude for whatever it is he chooses to bestow or share, and he—who has no less a need for unfettered professional camaraderie—quietly stores away little examples of perceived hurt and malice which, at bad moments, haunt him with the specter of friendlessness.

In the quiet of his house on the Hudson, feet up before a roaring log fire, Baryshnikov can look into the flames and observe bleakly that "there is not a hell of a lot of gratitude to be found in this business."

Surrounded by the cacophony of a crowded restaurant, two dancers—one a young corps member and the other a veteran principal—willingly tell of their own almost slavish gratitude for the changes he has wrought in their lives and their reasons for never telling the man himself a word about it. "It would be too much like sucking up," says the younger. "I don't think he really cares," says the older.

The younger was right, for Baryshnikov detests anything even approaching sycophancy; but the older dancer was wrong, because he cares desperately. Yet most of the means of promoting such a two-way dialogue are made difficult, if not impossible, by the hierarchical nature of a classical ballet company and the widespread but wholly erroneous perception of mutual indifference. This is the only secret of genuine substance in Mikhail Baryshnikov's American Ballet Theatre: that the desire to bestow gratitude is canceled out by the longing for appreciation.

Baryshnikov often broods about his men in ways far more complex than he does about his women. This is partly because he can think more coherently and naturally about men's dancing: Like his old teacher Pushkin, if words fail him he can simply show what it is he means. There are few male roles in the classical repertoire that he has not thought deeply upon, and for all of them he has extremely useful views. Anyone dancing the major male roles in *Giselle* or *The Sleeping Beauty* will get extended advice on interpretation, right up to the last seconds before the curtain goes up on the first act.

His resident troublemaker, principal dancer Patrick Bissell, was the cause of endless, sometimes nearly inchoate concern. For his wonder boy Julio Bocca, he takes a different line altogether and applies gentle goads to give him the mental energy to surpass what even Bocca himself thinks he is capable of doing. When Robert Hill, a promising soloist, was preparing to dance the prince's role in *The Sleeping Beauty* on the Met stage, Baryshnikov—perhaps sensing the weight of expectation that the young man was feeling—conspired to fix a part of his jacket, which probably needed no fixing but whose wearer certainly benefited enormously from this seemingly inconsequential bit of last-minute fussing. For a man thought by many to be inconsiderate, Baryshnikov can show the deftest touches of consideration imaginable when it comes to the business of others' dancing. Even when he despairs occasionally of the younger generation of male dancers, it has nothing to do with their lifestyles, but rather with how their mind-set affects interpretation.

"A lot of young men today, you know, are pretty insensitive," he said once after being annoyed when a certain dancer for whom he has great hopes treated his female partner like a sack of potatoes. "So many of the classical roles are built around a sense of awe for the mystery of women, and if the boy just ignores this because he doesn't even want to understand it, then it's a very hollow performance, you know. Something without a soul. An audience can usually tell. Many of our younger dancers—gay and straight—have trouble coming to terms with the sexual chemistry in the classics. It takes a lot of work to convince them that these classics may be based on fantasy, but fantasy is caught up in real human emotions and relationships. It's caught up in *romance,* dammit! They don't know very much about romance yet."

For a long time the outside world—even that part of it favorably disposed toward dance—simply assumed any male who danced must be homosexual. As Arlene Croce pointed out in *The New Yorker*, the biggest shock in Gelsey Kirkland's book for those with built-in prejudices against ballet was the number of beds of male heterosexual dancers she pirouetted in and out of. Inside the dance world, the complexities of the variety of male behavior were understood far better and for far longer than in almost any other endeavor in the West. It was understood, for example, that effeminate mannerisms in men did not necessarily denote homosexuality, any more than a robust, virile musculature and stage presence automatically indicated heterosexuality. In ballet, people were what they were, are what they are. Occasionally in the past, and increasingly again today, thanks to the AIDS scare, this matter-of-fact acceptance has been cited by outsiders as proof of moral degeneracy, rather than the recognition of reality that it actually represents.

As homosexuals in the United States started coming out of their psychological closets at the end of the sixties and throughout the seventies, it was not surprising to find homosexual dancers in the vanguard of "gay liberation," because they had been liberated on the quiet for so long and came from the least judgmental atmosphere in the arts. The emergence of AIDS as the major health scare in America during the eighties has been a setback to all this and is proving to be a major challenge to the dance world. It is an endlessly sensitive subject, fraught with misunderstanding and entirely tangible fears. Since AIDS is seen by many people as a disease that primarily strikes homosexual men, and since many of those same people believe most male dancers are homosexuals, there is an undue concentration of speculation centered on the dance world.

AIDS is the one and only subject on which no jokes are allowed at ABT, and when you consider the nature of some of the humor—both black and ribald—that rises up in such a high-tension and high-risk institution, that is an extraordinary statement. By the end of the 1986–1987 season, there had been two AIDS-related deaths inside the company directly and another peripherally. There is no longer much fear at ABT that its homosexuals are ignorant of the dangers involved in loose sex. As Ty Granaroli, a heterosexual, pointed out: "Most of my gay friends are either practicing celibacy or strict monogamy with a safe partner. . . . What I worry about are the heterosexuals—male and female—who consider themselves immune to AIDS and take very few precautions. If there is any fear lurking around here today, it is in this area, not with the gays."

Charles France and Mikhail Baryshnikov are the two chief AIDS-awareness gurus of American Ballet Theatre. For Baryshnikov, who has seen friends and acquaintances die from the disease, his work in raising funds for AIDS research has approached something of a mission—and this was a man who had hitherto shied away from taking any sort of stand, political or otherwise, in public. Yet as he observed the speed with which AIDS was working itself across the human spectrum, and particularly in the arts, he decided to assume a high-profile position. Since that decision several years ago, his work in raising funds for AIDS research has become a second vocation, often taking precedence over his own career. At its core, although he has never said as much, his deepest concern is for his own company—not for the contagion of the disease, but for the contagiousness of the psychological disarray the disease has caused. On this point Charles France sheds more light than the artistic director.

"It's a particularly emotional issue here," said France. "We are all obsessed with presenting an art that is life-bearing and positive, yet there are so many unreal elements to our lives when you consider that we are in the business of producing fantasy and magic and art. *Obsession* is usually the operative word. We are also obsessed at exploring art with no boundaries, and this ineffable, unfixed quality leaves its mark on our collective psyche. Just about everyone in the business is young, and most young people do not know very much about death, just as they don't know all that much about hunger and real poverty. At the most, they are required to imagine such things for the purposes of performance, but on the whole this is a hermetically sealed and protected world. Suddenly it was shattered by the whole AIDS scene. It may sound farfetched, but I would liken its psychological effect on young people to the Kennedy assassination in the early sixties. This business of unnecessary and inexplicable death is very hard on young people. It chills the soul and runs exactly counter to their exuberance for life. Dance is often thought of as a metaphor for that exuberance, so the intertwining of all this is complex and dispiriting.''

France realized, early on, the propaganda dangers implicit for his art and his company in the AIDS menace. The equation of a ''gay disease'' with a ''gay performing art'' spelled TROUBLE in capital letters, and he has been tireless in trying, wherever he can, to redirect and diffuse any direct association. ''The myth that AIDS is a gay disease is pernicious and destructive and must be fought with conviction and determination,'' he has said, more than once.

Baryshnikov echoes the same point: ''It's not just dancers who are dying, you know. It's writers and journalists as well, and businessmen and people in the armed forces. Anyone can get it.''

This is not the pair with whom to discuss certain harsh realities about AIDS, like the uncomfortably high incidence of transmission of the disease by anal intercourse. They know this, but the fact is not discussed, because anal intercourse denotes homosexuality, which brings it all back to ballet companies, at least around ABT. Someone—a reporter for *The New York Times*, for example—stumbling up against this extreme sensitivity can be in for a few surprises. When the *Times* assigned a reporter to investigate the effect of AIDS on the arts community, and ballet companies in particular, the rage felt within the community was instant. Many of the leading figures of the New York dance world were marshaled together to express their anger at such a ''blatantly prejudiced'' perspective, and it was Charles France who first framed the response. It was addressed to Max Frankel, the executive editor of *The New York Times*, but this version by France was never sent:

> My colleagues and I wish strenuously to protest the question we have been asked today by a reporter from *The New York Times* regarding AIDS and its relationship to homosexuality in the dance community.
>
> The issue of AIDS is deeply tragic and concerns everyone regardless of sexual persuasion or profession. There is a clear

implication in the question that the dance world's concern might be unique. This kind of intolerance is undeserved and unwelcome. It is as prejudicial as anti-Semitism, racism or any other form of persecution.

We in the dance community would like to believe that it is more important to educate the public to the facts rather than to invade the privacy of any individual, be he or she a dancer, banker, reporter, or file clerk. The question you raise perpetuates the mythology that AIDS is a homosexual disease. We are affronted that this question is allowed to be asked.

The letter was to be signed by Mikhail Baryshnikov, Jerome Robbins, Twyla Tharp, Peter Martins, and Lar Lubovitch. Peter Martins was concerned that the letter was both too defensive and too particular, and so it was rewritten but not before a few choice expletives were uttered by some of the other participating signers. In the end, such nuances will be lost on most people, for the final letter read as follows.

In response to the question raised today by a reporter from *The New York Times* regarding AIDS and its relationship to homosexuality in the dance community, AIDS is not a disease that discriminates. It affects homosexual and heterosexual men and women; it kills babies, children, and old people; it strikes down people in the business community, the arts, government—every profession, every age group, every sexual persuasion.

It is offensive for *The New York Times* to stereotype AIDS as a homosexual plague when it has reported extensively in its own pages that it is a disease that does not discriminate.

It is beneath *The New York Times* to pursue such an exploitative line of questioning.

At the heart of the AIDS tragedy in this famous company, then, is the implicit threat the disease makes to return ballet to the deadly old days when it was a specialist, high-society art, despised by mass audiences and considered vaguely effete even by its admirers. The image and hard-won reality of male self-confidence, which Mikhail Baryshnikov has done so much to sustain and enhance, is directly under fire. Herein can be found most clearly the reason for the Russian's passion on the subject. Because he is a ballet superstar who has transcended his own art, because he was prepared to withstand charges of "cheapening" that art by launching himself into popular entertainment, he may yet prove one of the more persuasive battlers for decency and tolerance that America has to offer during the AIDS plague. Of all the ironies, this one is the finest.

"I am a machine," said Jeremy Collins of Northampton, Massachusetts, who joined American Ballet Theatre in 1985, when he was eighteen years old. "I feel that here at ABT I have the best chance I will ever have in my life to succeed in dance. I have complete faith in Mikhail Baryshnikov. My admiration for him is total. His standards are the best, he is a strict perfectionist, and the thing he appreciates above all other things—above talent and beauty—is hard work. I know he was a fiend about work and about applying himself. He has absolute dedication to this business and I have no doubts whatsoever in my personal decision to trust his direction. If he says something I am doing isn't right, believe me, I will bust my ass to make sure it will be right."

Jeremy Collins is a handsome, earnest, eventually likable "machine" who can go on talking like this for a very long time. He is not being sycophantic, which is the initial impression left in all his talk about "Baryshnikov the man." In time, Collins convinces you that he has embraced a variation of old-time religion when it comes to finding the psychological props to sustain himself in the rigors of ballet. For him, Baryshnikov is the liege lord of the dance, and he would follow him unto the ends of the earth. The articles of basic faith come through, time and again, when he talks about the Russian. "I know he cares about the dancers," he said at one point, "even if he doesn't show it. You can tell he does."

Like many of the young men in ABT, Collins claims that he decided to become a professional dancer after seeing Baryshnikov perform. "He was my idol and he sustains me in my conviction to try as hard as I can to be a good dancer. I think he is the best director I will ever come in contact with. I don't care if he drives some people crazy. That is something wrong in them, not him. He has so much to offer. Just being around him is a privilege."

The tendency to smile inwardly when young Collins is cooing about his leader in this fashion is well known inside ABT. Collins is thought by some to be "strange" or "weird" and one is told not to take him altogether seriously. To do otherwise, however, would be a mistake, for in his adoration of the artistic director, Jeremy Collins has latched on to the chief commodity that—with talent—may provide him the means of vaulting out of the corps and into the front ranks. That commodity is obsessiveness. He doesn't merely want to be a principal dancer. He says he *will* be one. There is a personal agenda. And a niggling, ruling fear.

The agenda is awesomely simple. "If I do the things I am handed well, then everything will be okay. It is for me to be ready for all the challenges. They have started to give me some basic solo roles to see if I can take the pressure of being outside the corps. I feel I have the means to make a proper, fundamental assessment of myself, my work, and my talents. I will do everything to fulfill my potential. My training is good; my attitude is excellent. I have no doubts in my mind whatsoever—none at all—that I can achieve what I have set out to do."

This is one male dancer in the company who can see the merit and the cosmic logic of being cast as Puss-in-Boots in the final act of *The Sleeping Beauty*. It is not easy to be positive and enthusiastic about the role, because Puss-in-Boots is not such a great role. Collins, however, looks at the challenge "objectively": it gives him the experience of dancing in boots, which is "useful"; and, as well, "the characterization factor" is "crucial" in making an audience believe in his role. Did ever a Puss paw his White Cat with more dedication? It is hard to believe.

As for Collins's nightmare, it is not so strange when you consider the palpable ambition sustaining so much of his dialogue. He never worries about injuries, despite calcium deposit problems on one of his feet, and one or two other nagging physical woes most dancers are heir to. No, when Jeremy Collins wakes up in the middle of the night with sweat pouring down his brow, it is because he thinks he has somehow "pissed off" a key person.

"I don't know why it haunts me so much," he said, "but I really do dread pissing people off and getting people pissed off with me. Everything is very intense in a ballet company like this. I mean, this is the best company in America, so you better get it right here or another chance won't be coming. I dream about walking out onto a stage and suddenly not knowing what to do, and seeing the people who can make all the difference to my career glaring at me from the wings. This intensity, you know—it can be very, very exhausting."

*   *   *

Craig Wright, who was twenty-three when he joined the ABT corps in 1983 after dancing at the same level in several companies, including Britain's Royal Ballet, lives at the antipodes from Jeremy Collins, at least as far as his views on the artistic director and life in the company are concerned. A saucy, acid-tongued young Englishman, he embodies some of his countrymen's views on America. The dancers are "spoiled" both in terms of their pay and their status, and he finds their lack of understanding and appreciation for classical ballets "lamentable and laughable."

"At the Royal, the dancers are treated as ladies and gentlemen," Wright said, "but not here. Here the dancers are treated like children. It's like walking on eggs when you are around that greenroom (the artistic staff office) crowd. And let's face it, Misha is just not very bright in the way he handles dancers. You can't approach him. It's as simple as that. He doesn't know how to respond to ordinary inquiries or ordinary concerns. This doesn't help the atmosphere around here, believe me."

Wright's critical glaze is as misleading as Collins's zeal is candid. Like all top professional dancers, they are both required to be intensely self-focused. Wright, too, intends to break out of the corps, and at the time he was talking, he said that if he didn't make it into the soloists' ranks within two years, he intended to quit. In practically the same breath that he will pick apart ABT for some of its failings, he also makes a point of adding that "on the whole" it is a "magnificent" company and "by far the best"—at least in America.

Another outsider, but a very different sort from Wright, is Ross Stretton of Canberra, Australia. A principal with the Australian Ballet before he made the move to America in 1979, when he joined the Joffrey Ballet, he was hired by ABT as a soloist in 1981, and two years later was promoted to principal. He is tall and strong, and his fate in life—at least at ABT—has been to hoist big ballerinas, like Martine van Hamel and Cynthia Gregory. Stretton is an endlessly thoughtful, almost self-effacing partner, who provides rock-solid stability to a stage. He has built a relationship of confidence with audiences, but he rarely brings people to the edges of their seats. With the wry sense of humor that seems to be a personal hallmark, he says simply, "I make my living from putting up with temperamental ballerinas."

Yet Ross Stretton, who has a cool, low-key approach to life, also

JULIO BOCCA

PATRICK BISSELL

BARYSHNIKOV WORKING WITH JULIO BOCCA ON *DON QUIXOTE*

MARK MORRIS, TINA FEHLANDT, WENDY WALKER

ROBERT WALLACE, BARYSHNIKOV, MARK MORRIS

MARK MORRIS

ISABELLA PADOVANI, JEREMY COLLINS, ROGER VAN FLETEREN

TERRY ORR AND WENDY WALKER

Agnes de Mille (*left*) at a rehearsal of her new ballet, *The Informer*

MARTHA JOHNSON AND AGNES DE MILLE

relies heavily on Baryshnikov for inspiration and advice, probably in a more practical way than any of the other male dancers. He came to ballet relatively late, at the age of seventeen, after showing considerable talent as a tap dancer in Australia. His straightforward training at the Australian Ballet School and his easy rise through the ranks of the Australian Ballet did not prepare him for the hothouse of the intense New York dance milieu. His strongest memory of his first few weeks in the city was of wanting to get as far away from it as possible.

"I wasn't a great dancer and I was quite unprepared for the energy level in New York. It took me many years to come to terms with it all. Misha gave me a great deal of support. When he asked me to join the company, I said to him: 'You must understand that if you want me to do things, you have to help me—I can't just get it from watching.' Well, he has always given me that help, and I feel that I owe him a lot."

Stretton also has a considerable sympathy for the vagaries of Baryshnikov's superstardom. "I don't think his life is totally wonderful, really. Once, in a performance of Bournonville's *Pas de Trois*, Misha broke his toe on a landing and couldn't continue the performance. I was thrown into the role right on the spot. Because he is who he is, the story became a two-day sensation. It was really a story about him, but I was a crucial element in it, since I was the guy who had to replace him, and so those two days of absolutely mad media attention were indescribably wild. A nightmare, really. At one point during it all, he turned to me and said, 'Now you know what my life is like most of the time.'"

Even in a crowded rehearsal room, with all the dancers momentarily at rest, you could sense the presence of Patrick Bissell without being quite able to make him out. He was not a superstar, but he had a larger presence than any of the other male dancers. His aura was widely cast. Was it gamma rays? Vibrations? Electricity? Who knows?

Certainly not Patrick Bissell, who hated "all that analysis shit." What is known, what is incontestably certain, abundantly obvious, and even crystal clear, is that inside ABT, Patrick Bissell, principal dancer, caused more talk, more gossip, more anguish, more speculation, more anger, more conniving, more of nearly every emotion, than all the other dancers combined, including Baryshnikov.

"Look at him," said the artistic director to no one in particular, when he was watching Bissell dance extremely well one evening. "That bastard!

He can take over the whole damn stage when he wants to. You can feel the audience with him. Sometimes there is no one like him. Son of a bitch!"

Baryshnikov was not bemoaning the talent. Just the opposite. Watching this man-boy performing at top pitch merely reminded the Russian of all the grief he had had to put up with. This had been a troubled season for Bissell. During much of it, he was complaining of a variety of agues that kept him off the stage, while the artistic staff fussed and bothered about his future and speculated whether he was truly beating the terrible dependency on drugs and booze that had laid him low in the past. Patiently working with him, both Baryshnikov and, especially, Charles France had persuaded him to accept that he needed professional help. Charles Dillingham also became crucially involved and worked hard on the attempted rehabilitation. The company had got him admitted to the Betty Ford Clinic in California the previous year, and he had emerged five weeks later—"all cured," according to his own testimony.

There were people inside the company who weren't so sure, notably the physical therapist Peter Marshall. Bissell loathed and feared Marshall, calling him "a truly evil man," probably because the therapist was something of a whistle-blower on the problem of this dancer and drugs. But it was twenty-nine-year-old Bissell who aroused the most suspicions, suspicions that became tragic certainties at the very end of 1987 when the dancer was found dead in his apartment. During the season, though, the horrible business of retrospective logic did not surface and this mercurial, talented dancer led everyone on a merry chase. He canceled out of key performances at the last minute, turned up in civvies to chat up the ballerinas at performances he was supposed to be dancing in, drove Baryshnikov up the wall with his little suggestions for improvements to this and that, and generally caused such consternation that his fate within the company had become a weekly fixation.

"Oh, you know Patrick," said Ty Granaroli. "He's only truly happy when everyone's on his case, when he's got everyone turned upside down trying to figure out a new solution to the Bissell problem. I get the impression sometimes that the greenroom crowd get off on all the turmoil he causes. He may well bring them emotional relief."

On one level, the Bissell problem was perfectly straightforward. He was a gifted and extraordinarily exciting dancer who exuded dramatically potent danger on the stage. Offstage, his sadly troubled private life fighting addictions of one sort or another, brought him into conflict with his professional career. He liked confrontation, and tension, and being at the center of both. There is no one in the company Baryshnikov worked harder to sustain and help than Patrick Bissell, and no one who drove him to distraction quite so consistently.

"All the time with the girls, talking to them, performing for them," Baryshnikov complained loudly one day as he watched Bissell work a crowded stage prior to the curtain being raised on yet another performance he had canceled out of at the last minute. "He's supposed to be injured, dammit. It's insulting to the dancer who has to take his place. What the hell is he doing on the stage? Look at him. He can't stand still for more than two seconds. I'm going to get him banned from the stage. He's got to stop this. Charles. Charles. He shouldn't be here! *Charles!*"

Charles France lumbered over.

"Patrick has to leave the stage," Baryshnikov told him. "He's upsetting the dancers. I don't want him around. Get rid of him."

France took a deep breath. It is not a wise thing to ban principal dancers from their own hearth. He ambled toward the tall figure in blazer, jeans, and cowboy boots. "Patrick, you've been very naughty and I have to speak to you," said France, in playful camaraderie, and out of earshot of the artistic director, who was still fuming in the wings.

"Charles!" said Bissell, delighted to see him. "I was just going to come over to speak to you and Misha. I want to tell him—"

"Now you just stay away from Mikhail Baryshnikov right now. He's almost as jittery as you are tonight. I want to know why you . . ."

And France adroitly shepherded ABT's errant son off the stage and far away from the still smoldering Baryshnikov. If Charles France can be crudely and insensitively blunt at times, he also knows how to defuse bad vibrations like a master psychologist. In this case, France was as concerned about Baryshnikov as Bissell. It was France who pushed Baryshnikov to take the gamble and keep him on.

The next morning, in the artistic staff office at the Metropolitan Opera House, it was the turn of régisseur Susan Jones to be the house shrink in handling a difficult phone call from Bissell, who had become incensed after he learned he had been dropped from a cast list.

Jones is a serious, warm, and generous-hearted woman who has retired from active dancing and obsessive weight-watching. She understands as well as anyone in the artistic staff office the complex variety of emotions dancers have and has a special affinity with the corps de ballet where she herself toiled for so long. Unlike the ballet masters and ballet mistresses, whose main focus is correction during daily class and specific rehearsals, the régisseur has to set new or revived works on the dancers. Her phenomenal memory and ability to absorb the secrets of different choreographic styles made Jones a natural choice for régisseur, a position that requires her to organize all the rehearsal schedules and supervise the crucial architecture of the company's day. The always difficult business of balancing professional and personal problems, especially on the corps level, is especially weighted on her shoulders, and her patience seems something of a miracle—except with some of the more ego-saturated stars, where the tolerance level for hysterics visibly diminishes. With Patrick Bissell, however, she was very careful, knowing that egotism was the least of his problems. On this particular morning, he was being very complex as he complained incessantly into her ear through the receiver. Jones had already been listening to this almighty whining for nearly fifteen minutes when Bissell evidently moved into high gear. Finally, it had become intolerable, and she just held the telephone away from her ear. He was shouting so loud that his outrage could be heard by anyone within a few feet of Jones's desk.

"I won't goddam take any more of this shit, you know," said Bissell to Jones, who was quietly doodling on a pad as she continued to keep the telephone assault away from her ear. Only the tired, worried look in her eyes gave a hint of the despair she was feeling. "I have been busting my ass—do you hear me?—busting my goddam ass for this fucking company, and all you people can do is stay on my case, morning, noon, and night. You know, Susan, I'm wondering what the fuck I'm supposed to do to get a little appreciation from you people. Where the fuck does this jerk [Peter] Marshall get off saying . . . Susan? *Susan!* Are you still there?"

Background noise must have made it over the telephone. Jones put the receiver back to her ear, and with a soothing monotone worthy of a head nurse on a psychiatric ward, she said, "I'm right here, Patrick. I'm listening to every word you are saying. But honestly, Patrick, I think you are going to have to come to terms with . . ."

She shook her head back and forth as she listened again.

"Patrick," she said, her cheeks betraying a slight flush of scarlet, "that's a very offensive thing to say. I don't think I have to listen to that sort of thing and I think you should apologize to me. We are all working very hard in this office to get you dancing again. . . ."

He had hung up. She kept the phone receiver to her ear for a few more seconds, then, very gently, she replaced it on its cradle. "Patrick, Patrick, Patrick," Susan Jones muttered softly. "God help us all." She looked up, at no one in particular. "There's no getting through to him today. He's on another planet."

It even seemed that Jones might cry—not out of frustration, really, but in quiet lamentation. She didn't, though. She just sniffed rather loudly, poked around a pile of papers on her desk, and once again tried rejuggling some cast lists to accommodate Bissell's latest no-show.

Later that same day, Bissell begged off a face-to-face interview, preferring the safety of a telephone, but much of what he had to say was either rambling or simply incoherent.

"I need to feel trust," he said at one point. "I can't get any feeling of trust from anyone. I am permanently under suspicion. If they think I am going to take this bullshit any longer, they're crazy. . . ."

A minute later, he was talking about his relationship to Baryshnikov and how it had made all the difference in his life. "The thing I love about that guy," he said, all sequential logic hurled aside, "is the way he trusts my instincts. When I want to do something a bit different from what he thinks is right, he does me the fucking honor of giving my instincts some respect. Man, does that go a long way. . . ."

Three days later, Patrick Bissell was out of his civvies and into rehearsal clothes, working out with Leslie Browne in Studio A at the Met. They were rehearsing a difficult part of the *Don Quixote* pas de deux with ballet mistress Elena Tchernichova. Browne had been having a wonderful season. For several years after she starred in *The Turning Point*, she was dismissed benignly as a specialty dancer in certain minor roles. Two years earlier, however, Browne had been chosen as a first-cast Juliet by Sir Kenneth MacMillan in his own version of *Romeo and Juliet*. This season she had continued to transform herself into an extraordinary late-bloomer, dazzling audiences and critics with her fresh interpretations of the lead roles in *Giselle* and *Don Quixote*. There was pride in her transformation throughout the company. Fellow dancers turned out in the wings to watch her perform, and the artistic staff congratulated itself on its long-term faith and vision. Her self-confidence was charmingly manifest throughout the year and was being reflected on this day in the generosity of her patience for Patrick Bissell, who rehearsed the way some politicians campaign—with lots of busy bluffing, manic energy, and a mother lode of hot air.

"That's *exciting,* baby! Wow! Are you ever *fan*tastic!" said Bissell to Browne as they completed a sequence in the pas de deux. Elena Tchernichova looked over at the rehearsal pianist and they exchanged knowing, and somewhat jaded, glances.

"Okay, Patrick, what's your problem here? You keep missing the timing on the hold."

"Oh that," said Bissell, with irritated indifference. "It's my heel. It still feels like a knife is cutting into it. Anyway, I'm not important today. It's Leslie. Isn't she *terrific*! She has the most natural feeling of anyone I've ever danced with."

Leslie Browne laughed with affectionate cynicism. She, too, has heard the blarney before, but even so there was an element of pleasure in hearing it again, this time directed toward herself. She looked at Bissell as a mother would on a ten-year-old boy who had just said something both silly and affecting.

"Patrick, you're too much today," said Browne. "Why don't you do some push-ups and work off some steam."

"Good idea," said Bissell, who proceeded to do just that.

"No, Patrick! *No!*" moaned Tchernichova. "Not the push-ups. There isn't time. Patrick, please . . ."

It was too late. Bissell had started the first of sixty push-ups, and he hardly tired until he reached the fifty-fifth.

The ballet mistress lit a cigarette. The rehearsal pianist fiddled with her sheet music. Leslie Browne massaged a sore limb. The clock ticked. All danced attendance on the man-boy, knowing that confrontation would take even longer than patience. Forty-nine, fifty, fifty-one, fifty-two, fifty-three, fifty-four, fifty-five—"Now they're starting to hurt." Fifty-six, fifty-seven, fifty-eight—"Oh, God, let me get to sixty." Fifty-nine . . . fifty-nine and a half . . . "Nearly there". . . . "*Sixty!*"

"Okay, Patrick," said Tchernichova, "let's try that sequence again. I think Leslie wants to do it again."

Browne nodded vehemently. She would even like to do it again with the correct timing from her partner. He tried to oblige, but the alarming thought vaguely flitted through everyone's mind that maybe—this time anyway—his heel, or whatever, might actually be damaged.

"Oh, baby, you make me feel so *good* when you dance like that. That's really, really nice. Do you know how terrific you are?"

God help her, Leslie Browne blushed.

Dancers, and especially dancers at American Ballet Theatre today, are thought by many outsiders who follow the gossip columns to be wholly dependent on drugs. There is no evidence of that, only the melodramatic witnessing of chief offenders. Bissell's dependency on cocaine, which everyone in the company hoped he had licked after his stay at the Betty Ford Clinic, was so outrageous that it got him periodically fired. Kirkland's dependency, which she wrote about so frankly, produced the same result. When Bissell returned to ABT in 1985, it was written into his contract—a contract worded with the help of his dependency therapist—that he would be subject to fines (and, obviously, to being fired again) if there were repetitions. He went through all his fines in short order, and still the company fought to redeem him. Far from being typical dancers, he and Kirkland were in danger of becoming living scarecrows, symbols of the grave consequences of abandoning self-control.

A dancer or an athlete on drugs can fool people, even close friends, for a little while. They can even be seen to be doing better. In short order, however, the dependency becomes relentless and overwhelming. It is not just the missed rehearsals and performances. Sometimes the performances are not missed, and that can be even more horrific. In 1981, Bissell was so stoned he nearly dropped Kirkland, and dancers were desperately shouting at him from the wings to put her down. Life for everyone at ABT is on a fast track, and most employ common sense and even humor to deal with it. Others are victims. There are also victims who learn to cope and triumph. They have a tale to tell too.

"Well, it's true, people say Misha is the kind of guy who can kick you when you are down. But I'm a person he picked up. And believe me, I was way, way down for a long time. I'm someone he took a chance on, and I'm sure lots of people told him not to waste his time on me. Now look at me! I'm a perfect specimen of physical and mental health."

Despite the amusing bravado, Clark Tippet still doesn't find it all that easy to talk about the four lost years when he was high on speed and low

CLARK TIPPET

AGNES DE MILLE, BARYSHNIKOV, JEROME ROBBINS, AND PAUL TAYLOR
AT THE ANNUAL CHOREOGRAPHIC WORKSHOP PERFORMANCE

ROBERT WALLACE, JOHN GARDNER, KEVIN MCKENZIE, AND CLARK TIPPET IN A
WORKSHOP PERFORMANCE OF TIPPET'S NEW WORK, *S.P.E.B.S.Q.S.A.*

on everything else. Born in Parsons, Kansas, Tippet is the seventh of eleven children and he began his dance lessons at the age of five. He came to New York on scholarship at the age of eleven. Less than seven years later, he was dancing professionally with ABT and made a quick rise through the ranks to principal status during the fall of 1976.

In the official company program, it says that Tippet left ABT in 1978 "to expand his repertoire and performance opportunities," and although he did do some work during this period, he had also become—by his own admission—heavily dependent on "chemicals" to treat recurring depression.

"This is one helluva tough business, believe me," said Tippet. "The reality is very hard, and it took me a long time to come to terms with it, and the coming-to-terms was not a pleasant experience. I still have a problem talking about it. I guess I just went crazy and I got into a real rut because I came to believe I could not dance without drugs. It was a struggle to get back to normal and start assessing the reality of my life and profession."

Tippet's struggle did not go unnoticed by Baryshnikov. He has helped both friends and dancers kick all sorts of habits, and he keeps a careful check on his own drinking. This, and the example of the ruined lives he has observed, is threatening to turn the artistic director into something of a zealot on the subject of addiction in general, but not so much of a zealot that he does not know how to try to help at the appropriate time.

When he became convinced that Tippet was pulling himself together, he offered him a second chance with American Ballet Theatre in 1982. The gamble paid off in ways not even the artistic director guessed, for the reborn Tippet is starting to show signs of being an interesting new choreographer.

Now if there is anything a ballet company lusts after, it is a choreographer of its own. At ABT, classical choreography is the glue that holds everything together, but new choreography—built on classical technique—is what gets the company energized internally. It is not always appreciated by audiences, but new choreography—especially new choreography specifically created by a sympathetic artist from within the company—can be the most rewarding element in a dancer's life. Great choreographers are next to impossible to find, and the ones this century has produced can be counted on the fingers of one hand. Clark Tippet's debut work was to lead to others in coming seasons, but this first work— *Enough Said*— which was unveiled across America, was considered sufficiently interesting to see him placed in the category of "promising." His course was set for a considerably changed life, inside and outside the company.

Enough Said was originally commissioned for an ABT choreographic workshop, those useful off-season institutions in which artistic directors can reassure themselves that they are really not missing any hidden talent in their midst. Occasionally, but rarely, something of genuine merit emerges, and that was what Baryshnikov thought he saw in Tippet's effort. As for the choreographer himself, he laughed with a bit of self-deprecation, and said that he created *Enough Said* for dubious reasons.

"The season was over and I didn't have summer employment. I was broke. So here was three week's work and what the hell. . . ."

What he tried to do in the dance was show something of what he understands to be the nature of relationships, or at least relationships in his beloved New York City. He based *Enough Said* on his own experiences, many of them bittersweet, but perceived very knowingly. "There's a constant search in this town by people always looking for another person. To me the energy of New York comes from the tension between loneliness and searching—the two things feed off each other. There is great intelligence in New York, of course, but there is also a great emptiness."

When Baryshnikov decided to put this choreographic experiment into the main repertory for the 1986–1987 season, he didn't really think of it as a risk. It was an interesting and enjoyable dance that fitted nicely into a "mixed" evening. It would also take Tippet and his encouraging choreographic impulse right into the fray of audience and critical reaction. The audiences have been, almost without exception, enthusiastic. *Enough Said* clearly speaks to current moods, and people have responded generously and delightedly.

Among the critics, predictably, there was the usual array of instant judgments. With some, Tippet emerged almost on a level with Balanchine, which was as ridiculous as the weary paternalism of that dean of daily dance criticism Clive Barnes, writing in the down-market *New York Post*.

There was also a cruel review. After reading it, Mikhail Baryshnikov went up to Clark Tippet and put a warm arm around his shoulder. "Congratulations," said the Russian. "If the review was that bad it must be a hit."

Tippet was still a little wounded and wasn't taking in the sympathetic sarcasm. So Baryshnikov became less cryptic.

"Welcome to the club, Clark."

SUSAN JAFFE

ON THE ROAD

*L*ike the man without a country, American Ballet Theatre is a company without a home. To survive, the company must tour America each year and build up the idea that it has many homes, each with a theater, each with a little band of enthusiasts called the Friends of ABT, who try to buttress the institutional restlessness with a brief and illusory aura of the home hearth. In Washington, D.C., for example, ABT is "the official ballet company of the Kennedy Center for the Performing Arts," but the grandiose title means little more than a couple of short seasons annually. The city and the center cannot afford to keep ABT on a permanent basis, any more than Los Angeles can.

The 1986–1987 season, while perhaps the most momentous in ABT's recent history, for many diverse reasons, was utterly normal as far as the touring schedule was concerned. It began in New York in the autumn with six weeks of intensive rehearsals at the company studios immediately following the return of the dancers from the filming in Bari, Italy. Then, tons of equipment, sets, costumes, office files, dozens of dancers, administrative, production, and artistic staff members were dispatched to Orange County in Southern California to begin the annual tour. After two weeks there, the whole caravan moved a little bit north to Los Angeles and the Christmastime offerings of *The Nutcracker*. There was a brief respite for Christmas and New Year's before everyone reassembled in New York for two weeks of rehearsals and then headed down to two venues in Florida, Tampa and Miami. The intensity of the touring then became demonic, as it does every year. Florida was followed by two weeks in Chicago, then two in San Francisco, and a return trip to Los Angeles for three weeks, then back to New York for an eight-week season at the Met, followed by two weeks in Washington, D.C.

Although the logistics for each of these moves have been lived through many times over many years and, indeed, have almost become an art form, a major new production can bring major new headaches. During this particular season, for example, ABT was launching its lavish and heavily decorated new production of *The Sleeping Beauty,* as well as a new production of *Giselle* using the sets and costumes from the film. These had to cross the entire continent four times.

If the schedule is paramount in importance, requiring the most meticulous planning and the complete coordination of every single department in American Ballet Theatre, it also brings a degree of psychological pressure that is sometimes unendurable. Most of the seasoned troupers—dancers, artistic staff, and management alike—have worked out an accommodation to the schedule's incessant demands, but it is very hard on newcomers, who suddenly realize their lives are not encompassed simply by their rehearsals and performances, but also geographically, by their whereabouts at any given point on the calendar.

Living out of hotel rooms for half the year also engenders a profound sense of transiency, which is only marginally mitigated by occasional feelings of liberation. This life is very hard on marriages and close relationships. Although there are exceptions, the most successful are among those who have found partners from within the company. Dancers Amanda McKerrow and John Gardner, for example, are married to each other. Régisseur Susan Jones has found a sense of permanence with Lawrence Sterner, a production manager. And Florence Pettan, the wisest of the wise at ABT, laughs uproariously when she is asked if she ever contemplated marriage.

"Sure," she says, "contemplation is easy. Reality is something else around this place."

Everyone inside the company takes for granted the monumental volume of baggage that has to be carted around on the national tours, yet it still seems staggering. To start with the "small" things, both the offices of the company manager and the artistic staff have to be arranged so that a complete set of working files and office equipment (right down to paper clips) can be shipped off several days in advance and set up before the staff arrives, but still leave the staff with a functioning office back in New York. There are special touring trunks for these files, complete with drawers for letterhead and scratch pads. Because these items are all crucial for the day-to-day operation of the company, they have their own independent travel arrangements, which get them in place faster than the lumbering sets and costume trunks.

In his office on Broadway, Assistant Production Manager Lawrence Sterner sat at a computer and shifted imaginary two-ton pallets of equipment around the imaginary interiors of imaginary transport trucks. Sterner has to make everything fit and he works it all out on the computer, which is fed all the relevant information about the dimensions and weight of each pallet. A perfect fit does not necessarily mean a perfect distribution of weight. Watching him try to piece everything together on the computer reminds you of an intricate jigsaw puzzle, except that even when he makes everything fit, the computer may still tell him he has to redo the whole thing. Every single piece of equipment or item for the set has to be accounted for and accommodated. This might include additional lighting boards for some of the inadequate theaters ABT performs in, or the six golden cupids for *The Sleeping Beauty*, complete with their suspension cords and touch-up paint. There's no such thing as a last-minute addition: Schedules are too tight and costs too prohibitive for serious hitches.

The paraphernalia belonging to the costume and wig masters (or mistresses) is mind-boggling, starting with the most basic commodity of a classical ballet company: toe shoes—which at ABT are called "pointe shoes"—and slippers. The ballet toe shoe is one of the few instruments of torture from Catherine de Medici's days to survive intact into our own time. Its primary function is to assist female dancers in suggesting lightness—even weightlessness—to an audience. Unfortunately, it also assists in the rapid deterioration and malformation of the foot by forcing the entire weight of the body onto the forward toes. In all of classical ballet, there is no more distinctive, emblematic technical detail than dancing *sur les pointes*, and much of what we absorb from the art—its enchantment, fluidity, and grace—comes from this wholly unnatural action. So do many of the lamentable physical ailments ballerinas succumb to, from the small vertebrae of their necks and the discs of their lower backs, to the various bone distortions in their hips, thighs, legs, and feet.

It is not surprising, therefore, that the particular make of their toe shoes is very important to dancers. A principal ballerina will go through several pairs in a single performance, and each one has to be as good as the last. Ballerinas swear by certain makers: Freed, Capezio, and Gamba are the major firms. And it is not just the firm that is important, but the specific toe-shoe craftsmen. Cheryl Yeager, for example, only half-jokingly threatened to stop dancing when she heard her own maker at Freed's of London was retiring. A change of maker is as traumatic, in its own way, as a change of artistic director.

BARYSHNIKOV AND HELGA du MESNIL (BILLIE)

BARYSHNIKOV MEETING THE PRESS

CHARLES FRANCE AND SUSAN JAFFE

JULIE KENT AND FRIEND

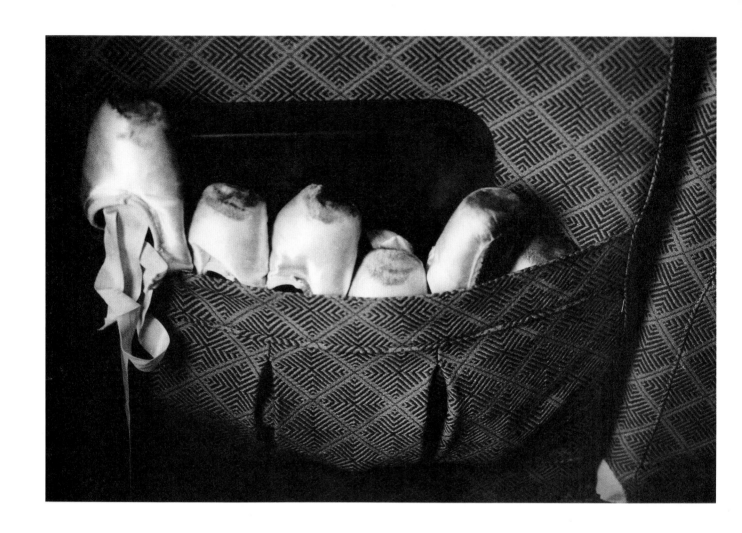

POINTE SHOES

The structure of the shoe, and its manufacture, hasn't really varied much for centuries. The sole is made of rawhide, onto which is sewed cotton-backed satin. This can all be done in a relatively routine way. The earnest part of the craft begins when the stiffened toe is created. Someone knocking a new pair of toe shoes with his knuckle would swear it was made of wood or metal, but it is only paper, paste, and burlap, built up in layers in exactly the same manner as papier-mâché. Later, a dancer's own sweat will soften the glue somewhat as the shoe gets molded onto the foot during rehearsal or performance. Toe shoes cost around $30 per pair, and every year ABT's female dancers go through 10,000 pairs. Just working out how many will be needed on tour is a major act of calculation.

The unending demand for toe shoes and the complicated logistics of moving equipment, while they are real problems, at least are concrete ones. A far more complex consideration is the extent to which the company changes character on tour. In New York, where most of the dancers make their homes, there is neither the same sense of camaraderie nor the same heated speculation and gossip as are found on tour. Group politics and relations are crucially important, and dancers are most particular about the people they will share accommodations with. If most of the dancers and the staff remain single and unattached, however, they do not lack resourcefulness in trying to bring a measure of stability to their touring lives. Clark Tippet, for example, has worked out a compromise. He is single, but tours contentedly with his beloved dog. There are a number of dogs who make the tours with their masters or mistresses, and it is easy to see why they become so important, providing as they do unstinting affection and a little of the ambience of home life in a succession of unappealing and anonymous hotel rooms. For ballet mistress Georgina Parkinson, a soft little ball of loving kindness that goes by the name of Basil even offers the occasional means of social reconciliation after a tense day of rehearsals. The ABT canine population often attends daily class, snoozing on the sidelines and only rarely getting into a scrap that has everyone howling on both sides of the barre. The dogs also mean that Lisa Weisinger has to find living quarters that will tolerate canines, which is not always easy.

To outsiders, the endless touring seems manic and alienating. From time to time it strikes the dancers in the same way. And yet, at ABT, this is their life, and it is accepted with fatalistic grace as a matter of course. The touring gives the company much of its distinctive profile. You can search Europe in vain—eastern or western—to find this troupe's equivalent; only history produces parallels: Diaghilev's Ballets Russes and its successors, of which ABT is one of the last living links. A large part of the specific energy of ABT is tied to its almighty touring schedule. No dancers in America or Europe are required to dance as often or in as many different venues, and they shoulder the task for the most part with remarkable fortitude and even courage. All things considered, the pay is lousy and—as we have seen—long-term security is a sick joke. Yet it is not merely mindlessness and brainwashing, or even simple necessity, that keep them all going. There is also a strong element of devotion—to an art, to an idea, to a concept of service—which gives this company the right to think of itself as unique. Any evaluation of American Ballet Theatre that ignores the daily sacrifices, great and small, made by everyone involved in its survival is flawed from the beginning. Everyone has given up something to keep the show going, and it is in the whole area of these sacrifices that you will find the only common denominator in everyone's lives, the only consistent element of egalitarianism which transcends the necessary but sometimes stifling hierarchy. It is what gives Florence Pettan the psychological resilience to stand up to the monstrous hours she is forced to keep, hours which inevitably leave her very little time for a private life. It is what gives Martine van Hamel the courage to continue fighting against perceived wrongs.

It is what makes Mikhail Baryshnikov nearly weep for the abject depression of one of his young dancers. It is what makes a lowly corps member feel he has a perfect right to criticize the lofty artistic staff. It is why Charles France feels aggrieved when his motives are questioned. Whatever any of them have gotten out of this art and this company, they have repaid doubly in one form or another. Only rarely are their accounts in debit.

None of this means that anyone accepts with grace the minor and major annoyances that such a massive artistic endeavor is automatically heir to. When it was decided to engage Sir Kenneth MacMillan to create a new production of *The Sleeping Beauty*, for example, any fool could have forecast some of the turmoil that inevitably ensued. The tale of American Ballet Theatre's new *Sleeping Beauty* unfolded right across their touring schedule: Much of the rehearsing was done on the road, dress rehearsals and tryouts were held in San Francisco and Chicago, and an inevitable crisis occurred in Los Angeles.

There were some dancers in the company who came to question the wisdom of contracting a new production of the most grandiose of all the classical ballets from the nineteenth century. No one questioned MacMillan's expertise. The ballet was in his blood from his earliest professional days, and with this latest effort he was eager to go back to the ballet's sources and turn it into the definitive production of the late twentieth century. As his wife, Deborah, said once during rehearsals, "Every single thing Kenneth has done in ballet has its roots in *The Sleeping Beauty*. It is here that he learned about structure and character. He believes passionately that the classics are not lost in the past and that one has an obligation to make sure they are bought forward in time, to address today's audiences."

In choosing this ballet and Sir Kenneth MacMillan to stage it, Baryshnikov made a major statement. The company already had a production of *The Sleeping Beauty* that was just over a decade old, but it did not say or display what the artistic director wanted in 1987. If he was building a company with the ambition of placing it solidly in the path of the full classical tradition, he wanted a production worthy of his vision. MacMillan represented Baryshnikov's best bet to connect ABT with a past that would transcend its own founding and hitch it to a new definition of the future. In the ballet world's version of apostolic succession, MacMillan can trace his right to mount a definitive new production right back to the first performance of *The Sleeping Beauty*. In the early postwar years, he was a young dancer with Sadler's Wells, the precursor of Britain's Royal Ballet, which restaged its famous 1930s production of *The Sleeping Beauty* mounted by Dame Ninette de Valois and Nicolas Sergeyev, the last régisseur of the Imperial Russian Ballet. Steeped in this production, he was aware that Dame Ninette was a dancer in Serge Diaghilev's Ballets Russes, which was the first, during its 1921 London season, to revive the ballet (under the title *The Sleeping Princess*) in the West following the Russian Revolution. From there, it was hardly a hop back to the Imperial Maryinsky Ballet premiere of Marius Petipa's greatest work in St. Petersburg on January 16, 1890.

Petipa, Diaghilev, Sergeyev, Valois, MacMillan—the link was very real. To reinforce it, MacMillan fulfilled his mandate from Baryshnikov by creating a sumptuous production and restoring many of the regal embellishments of the original production, including the final Apotheosis scene in which the entire assembled company, ostensibly paying tribute to

Princess Aurora, in fact celebrates itself and the triumph of grandeur. This ballet remains the definitive test of classical technique: The more faithful it is to its direct antecedents, the more rigorous and—if successful—the more rewarding the test.

With this new production, Mikhail Baryshnikov proclaimed that the goal of his American Ballet Theatre was equality with any company of the past, not only the ones of today. If, sometimes, his dancers didn't measure up to the gorgeous spectacle he had surrounded them with, they nevertheless had the full parameters of expectation erected for them—along with a precise accounting of the distance yet to cover. MacMillan's *Sleeping Beauty* was both a statement of arrival and a goad to work still to be done.

Baryshnikov was under no illusions that he would receive many thanks for this effort, either from the majority of corps dancers—who loathe the amount of sheer static attendance required of them onstage during the three-and-a-half-hour production—or the critics, who often use a new production of a major classic to strut their own stuff at the expense of all the labor and effort needed to mount such a ballet, demanding as it does the full range of a company's resources. On both counts, Baryshnikov was proven correct, and it was a measure of his steely determination to do what he thought was right for ABT that he paid very little overt attention to the sniping both within and outside the company.

"You shouldn't lie around on the floor like that. You will damage your costume," said soloist Michael Owen to corps dancer Loren Schmalle, who was gorgeously arrayed for a dress rehearsal in Chicago as one of the four foreign courtiers to the Princess Aurora in Act One. Owen knew a lot about the complications and expense of designer Nicholas Georgiadis's intricate costumes, since he played the character role of the king and had to parade around the stage wearing bolts of exquisite material in regal trains, crumpled ruffles, embroidered pantaloons, and damask tunics. Schmalle, on the other hand, was finding the whole business a colossal bore. As he lay scrunched up almost in fetal position on the dusty stage floor, he looked up contemptuously at Owen.

"I don't give one fuck about this costume and I don't give one fuck about this fucking production."

Temporarily at a loss for an appropriate response, Owen looked down at Schmalle and finally said, "Well, you should," and then turned his back on the disgruntled dancer. In the dozens of performances to come, Schmalle made good on his views. Whatever he was assigned in *Sleeping Beauty*, he danced with militant lethargy. He yawned his way through the courtier sequence and barely cracked a smile as a garland-wielding peasant. If you had seen him in nothing other than this ballet, it would be impossible to fathom what on earth had led him to this company and—even more fantastically—what the artistic staff had seen in him to find hireable. Later, when his pent-up anger was unleashed for an Antony Tudor ballet and the lassitude was burned out of him in a welter of psychological confrontations on the stage, you would find the answer. Like many of the younger dancers, Schmalle found the classics a tedious and empty exercise. He had not been brought up on them, as European dancers are, and unlike MacMillan, he did not see this extraordinary product of czarist Russia as the ultimate statement on classical technique, the high point in the tradition he had vowed to honor and safeguard.

As for the critics, they ranged themselves on various sides of the *Sleeping Beauty* debate. Many were wildly enthusiastic, and this coincided with a broad critical acceptance—after many frustrating years—for the direction in which Baryshnikov was taking the company. The all-important notice in *The New York Times* by Anna Kisselgoff praised the overall production for its lavishness and "unusual and soaring lyric[ism]." Nevertheless, in accordance with the broad dictates of human nature, the bad notices were more irksome than the good ones were pleasing. For flouncy airiness, *The Village Voice*'s Deborah Jowitt was hard to beat:

"If ballet companies were spoiled little girls, they'd always be demanding a new *Sleeping Beauty*. 'But your old one is perfectly good,' they'd be told. 'WAAHH! I want one with more lace and different names for the fairies, and pretty new steps like all the others have!' "

Baryshnikov's perpetual nemesis at the *Los Angeles Times*, Martin Bernheimer, found the production "somnolent," while Tobi Tobias in *New York* magazine decided ABT was in a deep crisis. "The gravest problem in *The Sleeping Beauty*," wrote Ms. Tobias, "is a desire for correctness that stifles both energy and musical response." Marcia B. Siegel, another senior member of the New York coven of dance critics, wrote in *The Christian Science Monitor* that "there are many oddities in ABT's new production of *The Sleeping Beauty*, but they are not the kind that add illumination to a celebrated classic. They don't even add up to the whole concept." Alan M. Kriegsman of *The Washington Post* paid due tribute to the production's "sumptuousness," but felt strangely cheated by its "lack

BARYSHNIKOV

CHRISTINE DUNHAM, BARYSHNIKOV, LESLIE BROWNE

LEOPOLD ALLEN WITH BARYSHNIKOV IN THE MAKEUP ROOM

CHRISTOPHER DAVIS

JULIE KENT

LESLIE BROWNE

LISA RINEHART

SUSAN JAFFE

CHRISTINE DUNHAM AND AMY GROOS

KATHLEEN MOORE AND LISA RINEHART

BARBARA MATERA AT WORK ON A COSTUME FOR THE UPCOMING
PRODUCTION OF *GAÎTÉ PARISIENNE*

CHERYL YEAGER

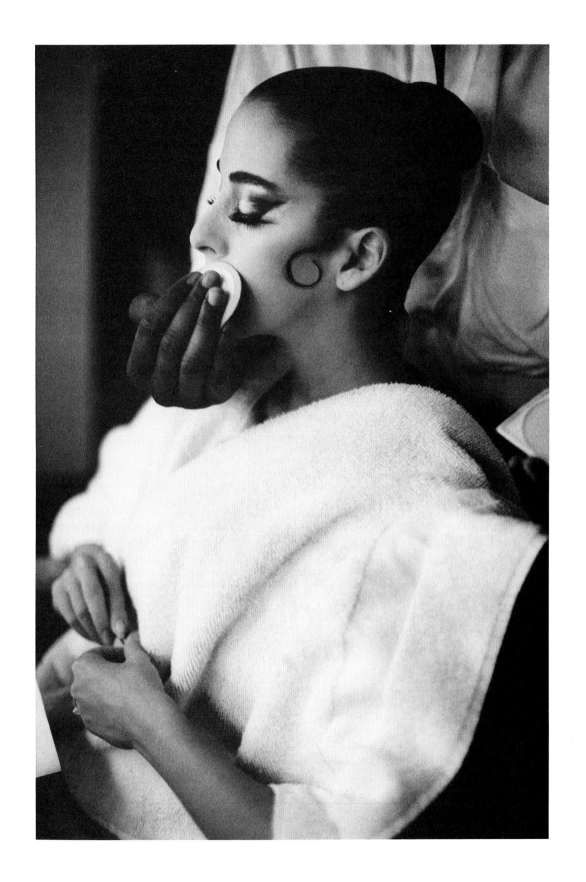

CHERYL YEAGER WITH LEOPOLD ALLEN

CHRISTINE DUNHAM SEWING POINTE SHOES

of heart." In San Francisco, a critic found himself snoozing off, while Clive Barnes of the *New York Post* amused himself with chastising MacMillan for what Barnes claimed was an inadequate credit list for his choreographic sources (a disputed point, as we shall see).

Knowing what was coming, it is not unreasonable to ask why Baryshnikov committed the company to a million-dollar production that found so few champions among the dancers and critics. The easiest answer is also the truest: He knew that it would sell out houses across America. And, of course, he was right. Because the classics are a reconfirmation of the enduring qualities of the human condition, because they speak directly from one age to another, because they remind us of concrete and long-established standards of excellence in an iconoclastic age, in short because they are classics, people the world over flock to them. The very same reasons for their appeal to audiences also make them appealing to artistic directors, because the classics provide the most tangible frame of reference for their own efforts. For the dancers, they represent a perpetual challenge to transform the strictest academic exercises into art.

His certainty that he was doing the right thing, for both artistic and commercial reasons, was more than enough to sustain Baryshnikov through the inevitable critical brickbats. As the annual Met season soared to unprecedented levels for advance ticket sales, he had reason to feel smug about his higher understanding of the value of *The Sleeping Beauty*. Heaven knows it was tested in other—less public—areas as well, not the least being in the troubled relationship between the company and its recently appointed artistic associate, Sir Kenneth MacMillan.

An important and highly regarded choreographer, MacMillan has a range that is comprehensive, from the lyrical, full-length *Romeo and Juliet* to the succinct theatricality of *The Invitation*. His special skill is for the brooding, dramatic ballet—the antithesis, in a way, of *The Sleeping Beauty*. Writing nearly two decades ago, the British critics Peter Brinson and Clement Crisp observed in *Ballet for All* that as a choreographer MacMillan was "the poet of passion, of dark, unhappy desires and frustrations and self-deceits. He can show us the gnawing appetites and needs, the loneliness, that polite Society masks behind its superficial behavior." These are also elements Sir Kenneth is quite capable of bringing to the back of the stage, when the curtains are closed and he is on the warpath.

The problem began as a malicious act of nature. Not long after the plans were laid to redo *The Sleeping Beauty* on the grandest scale, MacMillan was struck low by throat cancer. The news of his incapacity was a devastating blow. He had been experiencing trouble in his throat for over a year, but no one—including himself—thought it was as serious as it turned out to be. In the midst of an already hectic season, the most important in Baryshnikov's career as artistic director of ABT, MacMillan's doctors decided an operation must be performed at once.

It was inescapable, then, that Baryshnikov himself enter the fray and see the production through to its premiere in Chicago. Lady MacMillan was dispatched by her husband to keep an eye on everything, and she proved a model of diplomacy, talking only when asked her opinion and reliably supporting Baryshnikov on all public occasions. He reciprocated and often showed an unfamiliar humility in the face of the relentless demands of such a massive undertaking. He knew that Lady MacMillan was telephoning her husband several times a day during rehearsals, and whatever messages came back to him were treated with unvarying courtesy and immediate attention.

It was noticed by quite a few participants at the final dress rehearsals in Chicago that MacMillan's bad luck and Baryshnikov's response to it offered a unique opportunity to observe and contrast styles of artistic leadership. Where the Englishman had shown himself earlier to be all indirection and innuendo as he worked out solutions with the dancers, the Russian was now reinforcing his matter-of-fact and very direct approach.

"Ladies! *Ladies!*" Baryshnikov shouted at one point as the fairy godmothers made a grand final entrance in the Prologue. "You're hiding your charms. Spread out, spread out. Everyone give them some more room. They aren't cleaning ladies."

He seemed particularly concerned with one of the dancers, and although delays in dress rehearsals cost the company a lot of money, he went bounding up to the stage to speak to her personally and out of earshot of the large assembly of people who always gather for a major dress rehearsal of a new production. (The Chicago branch of the Friends of ABT had come close to filling a third of the theater that day.) MacMillan, on the other hand, humiliated dancers by sarcastically insinuating stupidity and lack of competence in front of their peers, as he proved when he returned to the company.

There was also the question of style. Baryshnikov was trying faithfully to execute MacMillan's wishes for the production, but his instincts in dancing style are to emphasize cleanness of line and dramatic intensity. At one point, when he was correcting some of the dancers in complicated ensemble work in the garland sequence, one of MacMillan's associates in the amphitheater turned to a colleague and said, "Kenneth won't like any of this. It's all too . . . too . . . too obvious."

MacMillan was not able to see his production until after the Chicago premiere. He caught up with it in Los Angeles and decided that "it was all wrong . . . crazy," and he hit the roof. He railed away without distinction at corps dancers and principals alike. There were ballerinas who could hardly mention his name later without virtually spitting it out. Extremely articulate staff members were momentarily left speechless: Even months later they could scarcely bring themselves to say anything about MacMillan's return and would mumble only statements like "very difficult—yes, a most difficult period." Some dancers were threatening open revolt and the static between the greenroom and the stage was heavy. Obsessed with his own vision of the ballet and, perhaps, a psychological compulsion to prove that without him the whole effort was a waste of time, MacMillan caused as much damage to company morale as anything since the cast list for Bari went up on the notice boards. Fortunately, or because the touring schedule takes precedence over even the gravest of brouhahas, the production settled down before the Met opening in the spring.

The great MacMillan crisis, as it eventually turned out, amounted to not much more than some quibbling differences of opinion over specific steps, lighting for the production, and "a bit too much clutter" in some of the densely populated scenes. Later, after Charles France had got his balance back, he would say sardonically, "Oh, thank God it all happened. It was far easier to see the Lilac Fairy once the changes were put in place."

Mikhail Baryshnikov, on the other hand, occasionally had trouble suppressing a grin when the subject of MacMillan's return came up. He would never say why, maintaining, right to the end of the season, that all honor was due to ABT's artistic associate. What clearly pleased him, however, was the full panoramic display the dancers received of another style of artistic direction. Most of them are very young and have had little, if any, experience of other companies and other directors. For them, the Baryshnikov style was not merely the definitive one, it was the only one they knew well. When, from time to time, they came to resent it, they had nothing much to compare it with. Now they did, and they didn't much like what they had experienced. It was partly due to a cultural gap. Accustomed to American egalitarianism and the familiar manifestations of Russian moodiness from Baryshnikov, the dancers were unprepared for the formal hauteur and withering sarcasm of a high British cultural magnate. They might have resented the occasional feeling of being cut off from Baryshnikov, but they had never before been treated like eighteenth-century peasants. The comparisons were odious indeed, and they moved Baryshnikov several notches up in general esteem within his own company. No wonder he was grinning. His studious exercise in humility and deference had repaid him handsomely.

A denouement of sorts came with an article by Clive Barnes that accused MacMillan of borrowing heavily from unacknowledged sources for *The Sleeping Beauty*. In a rage, the choreographer stormed into the artistic staff office at the Metropolitan Opera House with a sizzling letter he wanted dispatched immediately to Barnes's newspaper.

"It's dreadful, Kenneth," said Mikhail Baryshnikov, his features full of concern and fraternal support, "truly dreadful. You *should* write a letter. We never do, but go ahead."

By then, though, the ubiquitous packing crates were already being filled for the trip to Washington, D.C. The Met season was nearly over and it had been deemed a great success. Despite heartbreaking injuries, last-minute replacements, and the unending speculation about its elusive artistic director, American Ballet Theatre performed before more people at the Metropolitan Opera House than at any other time in its history. The usual variety of critical reaction was peppered this year with positive comments about an emerging style in the company. It was recognized that despite a number of injuries and the absence of important dancers like Jaffe (and the sporadic appearances of Bissell), the company had looked strong and cohesive. Moreover, other dancers, such as Leslie Browne, Cheryl Yeager, and Julio Bocca, had not only carried on regardless, but had done so in such a way as to reinforce the impression that this was a new and much more confident company than ABT audiences had ever before seen.

There was also something else that had happened, right out of the blue. The Soviets, in an unprecedented act, had invited Mikhail Baryshnikov to come home, if only for a short visit. Thirteen years after his defection, he wasn't all that sure he wanted to go.

BARYSHNIKOV WITH HIS DAUGHTER, ALEKSANDRA

LORD OF THE DANCE

The news came as it usually does from the Soviet Union—indirectly.

The artistic director of the Bolshoi Ballet, Yuri Grigorovich, was in America to prepare for an upcoming tour by his company. He had taken on the role of stalking horse for the regime and let it be known to the New York media that "Misha" —as the amicable cultural commissar called the prodigal son—had been forgiven and was welcome to come home for a visit. He let the media know within a few hours of informing the astonished invitee himself. The announcement was on the front pages of newspapers around the world, partly because of Baryshnikov's great fame but also, of course, because it was yet another dramatic sign of the changes in attitude being ushered into the Soviet Union by the new Communist leader, Mikhail Gorbachev. The article in London's *Daily Telegraph* on January 20, 1987, was typical of the worldwide curiosity about the affair.

A significant new aspect of Gorbachev-style détente was unveiled in New York yesterday when the artistic director of the Bolshoi Ballet announced that one of Russia's best-known defectors, Mikhail Baryshnikov, had been invited to dance again in his homeland.

Baryshnikov, 38, who has become the darling of the New York ballet world since his defection in 1974, was said by his manager last night to be considering the offer. The invitation to dance on the stage of the Bolshoi in Moscow was extended on Sunday night during a private meeting Mr. Yuri Grigorovich . . . had with the ballet star in New York.

"I've met with Misha and he will be dancing at the Bolshoi Theater," Mr. Grigorovich said at a press conference to announce details of the Bolshoi's four-city American tour this summer. But

according to Baryshnikov's personal manager, the dancer's answer to the Soviet invitation was, "Let me think about it."

And he did think about it. A lot. The unexpected and unsolicited
invitation sent him back in his mind to the time of his defection, when he
had also had to think out carefully what he should do and how it should
be done. There were profound differences though: Then, it was an emotional, daring decision of paramount personal importance; this time around,
the stakes were not as big, and the propaganda game initiated by Grigorovich
had about it some of the flavor of a chess tournament. It was a bold
opening move, Baryshnikov readily acknowledged, but then, in this kind
of a game he knew the difference between a rook and a knight, and it was
time for his move.

"I know them too well," Baryshnikov said the next day in Chicago,
where he was rehearsing the company. "God help me, I know them all
too well. We are going to have to play around for a few days."

Uppermost in his mind was the need to devise some way to regain
the initiative in the business. Although the invitation had come as a major
surprise, it would be considered churlish if he turned it down. On the
other hand, if he accepted too eagerly, it would look as if he craved
forgiveness. The Soviets had invited him to come alone to be part of a gala
performance just a few weeks in the future. He knew at the core of his
being that he had no intention of returning to any Soviet stage as an
errant son. In the delicate game that ensued, Baryshnikov's instincts told
him to allow time for speculation to build up, without any immediate or
direct intervention by himself. He has been adroit at deploying silence on
any number of occasions: following his defection, during some of his
famous disputes with leading dancers of ABT like Cynthia Gregory and
Fernando Bujones, amid the critical panning of *White Nights*, after the
Gelsey Kirkland memoir, and now here again. Silence is also his preferred
way out of most crises; even the most fevered speculation seems to him
preferable to the maze of dilemmas and woes involved in explication to
the press, "where they never really print what you tried to say anyway."

So the Soviet invitation was left hanging in the air. The trick was to
find a way of accepting that would put the Soviets on the defensive and
allow him to return to his homeland on his own terms. Almost from the
first day, he knew exactly what to do, but he smiled for a further eight
days before revealing his intentions. Even then he did it formally and

correctly, away from the prying eyes of the press. He told the Soviet Embassy in Washington to inform Grigorovich that he was honored and excited by the invitation, but that he thought it far more useful and suitable if he came with his company. "I am the artistic director of American Ballet Theatre," he explained. "That is my job and it is in this capacity that it would be most appropriate for me to return."

It was also in his mind that when he returned to the Soviet Union, he wanted his former countrymen to understand why it was that he had defected. He could best show this by presenting the full range of contemporary and classical works he had built up in his own company. In effect, he would be saying: "This is me, this is what I do now, this is what I couldn't do before, and now I hope you understand." The message wasn't new. He had made it in a more provocative and controversial way in *White Nights*. This was the film that was supposed to bar him forever from a return to the Soviet Union.

The most moving moment in a film that was largely mediocre comes at a quiet time, when the dancer tries to explain to a former lover and ballet partner why it was he defected. She has dwindled into a middle-ranking party official and chides him for succumbing to the lure of tinsel in the West. He can't explain his actions in words, so instead he says, "Watch me." In a very touching and direct scene, he proceeds to dance—without music—some serenely inventive modern choreography. The scene was missed by most of the film's nit-pickers, who concentrated on what they considered to be tasteless parodying of Baryshnikov's own life. Baryshnikov himself eventually started saying that there were some excellent ideas available which could have made the film much better, but "the director was determined to do it his own way." The idea of not being allowed to return to the Soviet Union bothered him hardly at all, but the distance between what he hoped to portray in the film and what was actually served up on the screen troubled him.

In talking to the Western press at the time of his startling invitation, Grigorovich alluded to *White Nights* and suggested that although Baryshnikov had been "a naughty boy," the film would not be held against him. This maladroit but precise reminder of the attitude of his old masters may have been responsible for Baryshnikov's zeal in playing the new game.

Once the gambit of bringing his whole company over was passed along the diplomatic route, "the fun really began," to quote the player himself. "I had to keep a straight face, really. This whole idea of me coming with Ballet Theatre came as a bit of a shock to them. Their first reaction was to say it was quite impossible because the Bolshoi Theater is to be closed for renovations. Well, we patiently had to explain that we had not requested the Bolshoi Theater. Hell, we could dance in a sports stadium or Gorky Park. You know, we are American Ballet Theatre. We dance anywhere.''

Suddenly, clouds surfaced over the negotiations. Communications with Moscow became difficult. Each pawn tentatively pushed forward from the motherland was nabbed by the errant son, sometimes with the clean sweep of the rook, sometimes with the devious retreating guile of a knight's move. In the end, he felt he had put the Soviet Union in check with an elegant two-pronged strategy: enthusiasm and innovation. In *The Washington Post* of February 12, 1987, Alan M. Kriegsman reported Baryshnikov's response:

> ''My hunch is that with a little good will on both sides, this can be worked out,'' Baryshnikov said yesterday in a printed statement. ''What every Russian knows is how to stand in line. I guess we have to stand in line to get a theater. . . . I felt that since the Kirov was here last year and the Bolshoi was coming this year, the appearance of ABT in the USSR would be the next logical step in view of our company's national stature and unique heritage in repertoire. The initial response from Moscow, as relayed to me, was enthusiastic. A few days ago, I heard of a communiqué—which was supposedly sent to me from Moscow but which never reached me officially—that ABT could not be invited because the Bolshoi Theater is closed in October due to renovations. I'm surprised, since this communiqué skirts the facts. The fact is that there are dozens of theaters in both Moscow and Leningrad other than the Bolshoi and the Kirov that would be appropriate. I never suggested any specific theater.''

And there the matter lay throughout the rest of the season. It was a significant event, but the Soviets never quite realized that they were dealing with someone whose emotional ties to his first country were no longer as strong as those he had established in his second.

The complicated invitation to return, however briefly, to the world he had left behind brought about within Mikhail Baryshnikov a very curious level of self-recognition, one he wasn't at all displeased to discover: He loved the United States, loved it with that special intensity of one who had long imagined and pined for this mythical nation, and then—miraculously—made it there. His sense of exile during the initial years had long since disappeared.

It was not just that America has offered Mikhail Baryshnikov the freest possible expression for his remarkable talent and industry, along with appropriate and tangible rewards. This was all wonderful, but it was something considerably less than what he called "the miracle" of his life. That miracle is "my American daughter," Aleksandra, born to the actress Jessica Lange in 1981. His relationship with Lange, from beginning to end, was played out in all the gossip and show-business personality magazines of the nation. They had, by his own estimation, some good times together, even if it didn't work out in the end. What did work out was the daughter, and the child has become the central focus of his ambition today. "Maybe I'm a lousy lover," he said once, "but you can't say I don't know how to make a beautiful girl."

Aleksandra Baryshnikov now lives with her mother, stepsister, and stepbrother, visiting her father regularly throughout the year, either at his house on the Hudson or wherever he might be on tour. They have ecstatic reunions, but within a few days he experiences the standard frustrations of an absent father who is not all that adept in entertaining a seven-year-old child for hours on end. But the same child nevertheless represents his most tangible attachment to his new country and his new life. He has found that his existence has a purpose beyond even his commitment to his art.

Once, when Aleksandra was a baby and he and Jessica still lived together, the infant fell off a table. It was not an uncommon experience for young parents, and neither was the subsequent reaction. "We held her, Jessie and me. We held her together. We could not stop crying. The baby was so helpless and so fully dependent on us and of course we felt terribly negligent. But we also learned at that moment how incredibly precious she was. She was so tiny, my daughter, but I never had such a strong feeling about anyone before."

So, in the end, Mikhail Baryshnikov has discovered that he is the father of Aleksandra Baryshnikov, and this, it seems, may well be paradise enough for the boy in the Riga train station whose mother, in every memory of her, keeps receding from his grasp.

*   *   *

"He's okay, you know," said Olga Evreinoff. "He's not perfect, but he's not so bad either. I don't really know much about the Gelsey business. I feel she was badly used by many people, but mostly by herself. Yet Misha, you know, he's not this terrible person she wrote about. He's just Misha. He's a nice guy and very bright. He's a good friend. I mean, he's a friend you can count on when trouble comes. These things aren't so unusual to say about someone, I guess, but in his case they are true, and so many people say so many things about him that it comes as a shock to discover his normalcy. He was fun to be around when he was a student. He still is."

Baryshnikov and Evreinoff were students together in Leningrad, although she made it to the West several years before him and in a less ostentatious way. Married with two children, and based in Ottawa, Canada, she now free-lances as a ballet mistress for several companies and had been contracted by Baryshnikov to work with American Ballet Theatre for several months during the early summer of 1987. The two are very comfortable together, although mutual friends say there is less intensity in their warm friendship than there is in the other great Russian relationship he has, with the Nobel laureate poet and writer Joseph Brodsky. Evreinoff, however, probably understands him better. She smiles as she listens to analyses of Baryshnikov's character that cite complex motivations for his moods and actions.

"Haven't you noticed," she asked quietly after one such exposition, "that the most complex quality of Misha is how uncomplicated he is? He has simple pleasures and normal needs. He is a very sane artist. If his relationships with women seem, well, strange, consider his condition and life. They don't seem so strange then. What is remarkable is his continuing faith that companionship and trust are possible."

On a warm June day, Baryshnikov and Evreinoff traveled to Glassboro, New Jersey, along with several other friends, to see a contingent of dancers from their old Leningrad company, the Kirov, perform during a low-key tour of the eastern United States. The trip was a revelation on several fronts, especially since it came after the invitation from the Soviet Union had been made. The two friends on the road to Glassboro were in a wildly nostalgic mood for their past. Indeed, there were those in the group who thought the pair had become somewhat florid in their memories of the Kirov. "Well, at least with these dancers we will see consistent style and good schooling," Baryshnikov said as he waxed poetic about the undoubted superiority of certain aspects of the Russian ballet system. He was also in an expectant mood because he was about to see his famous former partner, Irina Kolpakova, who had been with him on tour when he defected.

The outing was also an emblematic encounter with the perils of stardom, a normal occurrence for Baryshnikov, but always something of a shock for anyone in his entourage who has never experienced it. Unannounced though his presence was supposed to be, his appearance at Glassboro was anticipated by various news agencies, which had been tipped off by local promoters anxious for maximum press coverage. There were at least fifteen reporters and television journalists on hand, staking out every entrance to the local theater. Baryshnikov and his friends arrived about fifteen minutes before the performance was scheduled to begin. He was spotted the moment he got out of the car. Cameramen with portable video equipment started toward him at the gallop, microphones appeared out of nowhere to loom a menacing inch from his face, and other people ran toward the scene from all directions. He smiled at everyone, but never stopped for a moment until he got inside the theater.

In the lobby local worthies assembled from thin air and formed themselves into a reception line he had to go down. At the end of it, a local artist presented him with a portrait, done on black velvet, of himself in grotesquely suggestive tights. The television cameras and news photographers had followed him in and continued the pursuit right to his seat in the auditorium. They set up at a spot three rows in front of him. People already seated stood up to see what the commotion was all about. Within ten seconds you could hear the single word "Baryshnikov" buzzing all over the place.

At least a dozen people pretended to have seats in his row and barged past other seated audience members until they were directly in front of him, at which point they looked at their tickets and said, "Oh, my goodness, this must be the wrong row. . . . Well, well, if it isn't Meekhill Bershcropp! *How are you?* I was just saying to my husband, I wonder if you are going to be here tonight, and . . . well, here you are! Oh, I wonder if you would mind autographing this program. It's not for me, but my little girl [granddaughter, girlfriend, fiancée, wife, mistress, mother-in-law, maiden aunt, schoolteacher, invalided sister] would be so thrilled to have it. I hope you've got a pen. You don't? Fred, Fred, *Fred*! Have you got a pen? Meekhill needs a pen to sign this program. . . ."

They are certainly not terrible people, and on his better days he knows this and makes his version of an allowance for the vagaries of human nature and the abnormalities of his celebrity status. They are people who find themselves in the presence of a major icon who has become so familiar that they have come to believe he is a part of their own lives—who *is* a part of their lives, but has not been acquainted of this fact until the moment of direct contact.

Baryshnikov happened to be in a good mood that evening, and so he was able to take it all with good grace. His experience has given him wisdom in dealing with potential hysteria, and he is positively ingenious in coping with most exigencies. At Glassboro, for example, he quickly scouted the auditorium, noting within two minutes that the closest exit led directly to the main lobby, but a slightly farther one gave out onto an anonymous corridor where there was a doorway leading directly to a parking lot. He made an unostentatious point of talking to groups of people in his row whom he might have to get past quickly and won them to his cause with the help of the ever-present cameras clicking a few feet away.

"They [the media] must make it very difficult for you to get around," said a pleasant, gray-haired woman as he went past her to regain his seat.

"Oh, it's not so bad if you can run—so watch your feet later if I come past you fast."

She smiled at him as if he were her long-lost son: "Please! Step on my toes! It would be an honor."

Trying to get Baryshnikov to account for the variety of his crowd appeal is not easy. He has still not come fully to terms with the intensity of so many people's desire to peer into his soul, and the often bizarre and sometimes dangerously unreal public life he leads. Even today, when he is forced—and that is the correct word—to give an interview about his plans for the company and his own views on cultural controversies, he seems to see it as a species of playacting.

"You know, in Russia, this business of exposing yourself if you are a famous person is just not done. When I first came to America, people kept on asking me what I thought about this or that, what were my impressions of modern dance, what excited me about American culture. You know—even what kind of salad dressing do I like, and is it true I do not wear underwear, or something completely crazy like that. But I was trained just to be a dancer and not to have an opinion, so it was very, very hard for me to come up with all these instant answers. I could not understand why so many people needed to know so many things about my life or my outlook. I was a very typical dancer in that way. I just want to say that all my answers are in my dancing. Watch me and you will see what sort of things I think, what sort of human being I am."

He enjoys playing the celebrity game up to a point and has learned the main rules. He knows when and where to be seen; he knows how to keep the gossip columnists contented without actually pandering to them; he can exhibit his charm instantly if he can be convinced of its genuine need. And, if he is not convinced, which is often, he knows how to say "no comment" and make himself scarce.

Some women—and an alarming number of men—would quite literally fling themselves at him. Back in the main administrative offices of American Ballet Theatre, some of his faithful but not fully reverential staff have kept a scrapbook of the solicitations that come to him with nearly every mail delivery, complete with suggestive photographs, pertinent dimensions, and hours of availability. He has never been shown it, or at least that is what is said.

The scrapbook is a random directory of young females who are sure that their futures encompass a major encounter with Mikhail Nikolaievich Baryshnikov. Here was "Dawna" from Hawaii, with a degree in sociology. She was lying in an undeniably suggestive position on a sunbathing chaise. Her hair was blond. Her features were pleasant to encounter and were clearly discernible under the wet bathing suit. Neatly typed out was her address, phone number, and instructions on what to do if a man answered. On another page was "Susan" from Texas. Susan was appealing to what she was sure was Baryshnikov's adventurousness. She was six foot two, and although he was somewhat shorter (about five foot eight), she was "really certain" he would be interested in the "extra dimension" she offered to his curiosity. She herself was turned on by "little men with big ambitions." They came in all sizes and colors, from most of the states of the union, and from countries far away. The only fan letters and photographs the staff ever allow the artistic director to answer personally come from ballet-mad little girls. For them, there is always some sort of acknowledgment.

He has presiding fears, some of which are directly related to his celebrity status. Crowds, and the threat of being trapped by them, form a

BARYSHNIKOV RECEIVING AN INDIAN CEREMONIAL HEADDRESS

BARYSHNIKOV AT AN EVENT IN HIS HONOR

dominant motif. Within two weeks of his defection in 1974, for example, he went on his first public outing in Toronto, to watch a professional tennis tournament. To his horror, his presence was announced over the public address system and within a few minutes he was surrounded by overexuberant well-wishers. Today, he knows how to walk quickly on the streets and keep his head down.

Still, there are very ugly way-stations in his life, including occasional death threats, and one, during the 1986–1987 season in Florida, was sufficiently serious that he needed special protection. Once, when he turned down a request to autograph a program because the sight of him with a pen can create an instant crowd, he got a great gob of spit in his face from an outraged woman.

In the Soviet Union, one of the undoubted perquisites of Mikhail Baryshnikov's stardom was the quantum leap in privacy he was ensured, which separated him from the all-encompassing scrutiny of neighborhood committees and petty officials that is the lot of ordinary people. In America, such automatic privacy is reserved only for the ordinary, since part of the price of being a celebrity is forswearing the right to walk unmolested down the street. Such solitude as is available must be purchased: in homes with ample and secured grounds, and by hiring personnel whose job it is to find a niche of privacy for their employer—all of it at great cost.

There are very few areas of Baryshnikov's life that are not cluttered with the consequences of his stardom. Not all of it is negative, of course. His name endorsing a product earns him money. His reputation is all the cachet necessary to gain entrance to the White House. He commands the respect—or, at the very least, the curiosity—of wealthy businessmen, publishers, movie producers, writers, impresarios, agents, politicians, university presidents, and the entire world of fellow celebrities. The pull of such a world of achievers and luminaries is intense, partly because in their company he can be more relaxed, knowing that many of them experience what he experiences. The major quality in his nature that keeps him from being swept up entirely by the *haut monde,* however, is his insatiable curiosity about so many aspects of life that lie beyond his professional world. As a keen fisherman, he has an uncomplicated entree into the world of worms and hooks and long, brooding, satisfyingly quiet sojourns on rivers and lakes. His love of literature and politics leads him down all sorts of strange byways, while an internal sensory system—alive to all the nuances of contemporary and popular culture—ensures him a life beyond ballet that is wide open to opportunity.

"This is how I live," he said matter-of-factly as he walked around the grounds of his house on the Hudson. "It's me, and Tim-the-dog, and Billie, and the house. The house is my refuge and Billie is my good friend and Tim-the-dog is crazy."

Well, not really crazy, just a little exuberant. Tim-the-dog has mixed parentage, but there was a German shepherd somewhere in his ancestry. As a young mongrel he was cruelly treated, and Baryshnikov adopted him when he was all skin and bones and nursed him back to health. The beast's utter affection is never unwelcome, and he is totally passive when being chewed out by his master. Unlike the master, he never sulks.

Billie is the former Countess Helga du Mesnil-Adelée and she lives at the house on the Hudson, which she has largely decorated and where she keeps a home for him. The house is small by the plummy, overstuffed standards of his neighbors. Outwardly, you would call it a cottage, with its clapboard siding, wide, covered veranda and deck, and gabled second-story windows over the front door. The house sits in three acres of garden and woods overlooking the river near the verge of a steep bank. Half of the property was only recently purchased and contains a wonderful stand of white birch, a tree that strikes deep into the soul of any transplanted Russian.

Inside, Billie has pulled off something of a miracle. She has managed to retain the simplicity of a New England cottage while transforming the principal room downstairs into a fair facsimile of the living quarters of a Russian *dacha*. The dark wood paneling, simple chairs, random icons, colorful ballet costume sketches, small landscape oils (for which he has a passion), stone fireplace, and books coming out of every cranny, provide a warm, intimate, and knowing ambience that clearly soothes Baryshnikov's soul whenever he enters it. It is Billie who has already laid the fire and got it crackling on a cool summer night. It is Billie's cooking you can smell from the kitchen. It is Billie who picked the flowers from the garden and arranged them all over the house.

Older than Baryshnikov by more than a decade, Billie has been around as a friend for nearly eight years. The former wife of a titled

LISA RINEHART AND BARYSHNIKOV

CLOCKWISE FROM LEFT: JOHN FRASER, OLGA EVREINOFF, LISA RINEHART, AND BARYSHNIKOV AT HIS COUNTRY HOME

BARYSHNIKOV WITH TIM-THE-DOG

BARYSHNIKOV

BARYSHNIKOV WITH TIM-THE-DOG

French diplomat, she was born in the immediate prewar years in Germany and has borne much grief in her life with stoical endurance. She has a remarkable capacity for self-abnegation, and her humility, while never sycophantic or pathetic, is her most notable characteristic. She talks openly about having had a terrible struggle to fight alcoholism, and she accords Baryshnikov gratitude for the part he played in helping to win the battle. Billie is not exactly a mother-figure to him, but then again, she's not far from it.

"I never ask him about his work. I never read reviews about his dancing or his movies or any of that stuff. My God, for a long time I may have been the only person who never saw him dance. But I knew that he needed a completely reliable, calm home—his home—and this is one thing I absolutely knew I could provide. So this is what I do. His home is also my home. Our friendship is quite, quite pure. We know what we need from each other, and we give it naturally. He needs the security of a home and a refuge from his work. I need the security of a home, too, and the knowledge that I am actually needed."

That she is needed, there can be no doubt. It is not simply the creature comforts, which she either provides personally or arranges for him—from repairing legwarmers to managing this property and the elegant loft they also maintain in Manhattan. There is also an element of quiet comfort the two draw from each other which mitigates the various and vicarious depressions and private griefs they both succumb to from time to time. It is no more a smooth and uncluttered relationship than any intense friendship anywhere, but it does transcend the complications of his flirtations and affairs, largely because of the generous and unfettered simplicity of Billie's soul. In May 1987, Baryshnikov said, "I cannot live with American women. God help me, I've tried, but it has never worked out. I can live with Billie—that's who I can live with." A few weeks later, he and Lisa Rinehart had worked out yet another sort of mutual accommodation and they were a team again. Rinehart is far too wise a woman not to realize the stability Billie brings to his life, and both women are careful to stay clear of each other's perceived territory.

Not surprisingly, there have been adjustments made over the years in the relationship between Baryshnikov and Billie. In the earlier years his dark moods troubled her terribly. Because of her gratitude to him for the help he provided in fighting her alcoholism, she felt frustrated at not being able to assuage his periodically enveloping gloom, which sometimes simply overwhelmed him. To all such mothering advances, she said, "He would turn himself into stone." Eventually, Billie accepted that the depressions were a part of his character that she could not alter. As his dancing days grew shorter and further between, so—in almost direct proportion—did his ability to control the moods.

"You know, for several years we just never talked about his dancing or anything to do with his career. If he was on television we would never watch it, because I would never know he was on some show. I would hear about it from friends or neighbors. This was not something to be questioned. This was a fact of our lives and I learned to accept it. Then one day he said to me—right out of the blue—'Hey, Billie, you want to see this bullshit I do every night?' And, you know, I could feel the tears coming, but I fought very hard so he could not see them. So I just said, 'Yes, Misha, I would be very honored to see this . . . this bullshit you do.' And then I went to my room and cried the whole night. He never knew. I never told him."

From this sweet honesty, it should not be taken that Billie is so totally caught up in selflessness that she lacks a personality. It is simply that her single-mindedness can be akin to a force of nature. Once, Baryshnikov's neighbor, actress Margot Kidder, came calling with her weekend guest. Billie and Misha both like Kidder, but Billie got it into her head that Baryshnikov needed some protection from unexpected callers. She had been working in the kitchen when the twosome arrived and she went to the front door in a great act of bustle and busyness. "No, no," she told Kidder and her companion. "Misha is out." (He was sleeping and knew nothing about the visit.) No, she didn't know when he'd be back. Yes, she would tell him Margot had come calling. Kidder's companion looked vaguely familiar, but Billie was all efficiency and goal-oriented. Baryshnikov's sleep was not going to be disturbed. It wasn't till she watched them trudge back across the property that she realized who she had sent packing. It was the Prime Minister of Canada, Pierre Trudeau.

A few years later, during the early summer of 1987, her car stopped at a red light beneath an overpass on a drive back from the house on the Hudson to midtown Manhattan. A number of kids emerged from seemingly nowhere with water sprayers and cloths to clean windshields for a few coins. In addition, a lurching wino ambled among the temporarily halted vehicles with no services to offer save the retraction of his outstretched hand once he had received some money. He made a mistake approaching Billie's car.

"Gimme a dollar, lady. It's not much for you."

Billie looked at him with pure affection, ignoring the violent breath and disgusting clothes. "I know you," she said.

"Lady?" said the wino.

"I know you. You're me. I was like you. That bad. You can shake it off, because I did. You have to fight very, very hard, but you get your life back. That's worth it. You can do it. As bad as you are, you can do it. I did it! I was as bad as you!"

The traffic signal had changed and a few drivers were impatient and began tooting their horns. They might as well have been in the outer antipodes as far as Billie was concerned. Drivers whizzed by on the outside lanes and the impatient ones behind Billie started to pull out, shaking their heads with that special contempt New Yorkers have when they have been personally inconvenienced. Billie was oblivious to it all. The wino had retracted his hand, assuming that all he was going to get was a lecture, but as she railed away at him she was fishing in her purse and eventually came up with a five-dollar bill.

"I know you will spend this on liquor," she said, "but you don't have to. You could get a bit of good food. But if you buy liquor, try and remember you are buying it with money from a person who has been like you and who won the fight. Just like you can if you really try."

In his house on the Hudson, Mikhail Baryshnikov keeps very few of the trinkets or mementos of his career. There is no collection of photographs of him at famous moments or with famous people. There are no framed awards or distinguished citations. Other than a collection of ballet books, some of which mention him, there is virtually no hint that a dancer is in residence, except for the occasional dancing slippers—bruised and crumpled from overuse—which he uses for bedroom slippers from time to time. He has no special little studio to do his daily exercises at the barre (if he is not going into town to do them at the ABT studios). Any old thing to grip on to will do: in summer, the veranda railing; in winter, a bookshelf or the back of a chair. He makes no fetish of necessity and, in fact, groans as he goes through the exercises. "I hate it. I hate every minute I have to do this goddam stuff. I long for the day when I no longer have to do it.

My body longs for retirement. My mind longs for it. It has been like this for several years. I hate it.'' But he does it, and will keep doing it right up to the day he makes his final, complete break from the dancing stage.

The one place in his house where there are reminders of his nondomestic life is on the refrigerator, but here the effect seems mostly to be one of self-mockery. It is an eclectic assortment of trivia: an invitation to the White House for a dinner in honor of Princess Margaret of England; a nude beauty from Hawaii circa 1950; a collection of random postcards featuring, variously, Marilyn Monroe, the ballerina Alexandra Danilova, Fred Astaire, the Sphinx, Stalin holding a pussycat, ''Indiana Jones'' inside the Temple of Doom (with Baryshnikov's face pasted on top of Harrison Ford's), James Cagney as a young man, James Dean, Nijinsky in *L'après-midi d'un faune*, Sitting Bull, a trio of very fat ladies on the Riviera, and Einstein; and finally a picture of himself, shirtless and dressed in riding breeches, standing in front of his own refrigerator.

''[Joseph] Brodsky tells a wonderful joke about all the changes for the better in the Soviet Union,'' Baryshnikov reported one night as he relaxed in front of a fire Billie had laid and lit. ''There was this poor intellectual during Stalin's time who was told by the party that two plus three equals seven. He knew he should keep his mouth shut, but he was young and reckless so he pointed out that two plus three doesn't really, you know, equal seven. It equals something else. Well, of course he was arrested and sent off to the *gulag* and kept there for years and years.

''Finally, the great day comes when a new regime is installed at the Kremlin and he is released and rehabilitated. On the first day of his freedom, he learns that the new regime has decreed that two plus three equals six. He's still the same man. He just can't help himself, and so he tells to anyone who will listen that, in fact, two plus three equals five. Very quickly, the KGB make a little visit to his home. 'Comrade, comrade,' they say to him, 'come to your senses. Be reasonable for all our sakes. You don't want to see a return to the bad old days when two plus three equaled seven, do you?' ''

He laughed at this retelling of a favorite joke, for he adores black humor. He also adores popular entertainment, both watching and performing it. His forays into this world—television specials and movies, in particular—have won him no friends among the ballet cognoscenti, but then he has always rather enjoyed doing precisely those things that leave his most tasteful admirers appalled.

For those who saw him as a classical purist, he embraced the unusual and controversial virtuosity of the exciting contemporary choreographer, Twyla Tharp, thereby identifying himself both with the prince in *Swan Lake* and the cocky male in *Push Comes to Shove.* For those who loved him for his daring in embracing the latest in contemporary choreography, he went onto television and enjoyed himself thoroughly in flashy specials celebrating Hollywood and Broadway. "The fervent enthusiasm with which he [Baryshnikov] discussed these programs with me," wrote a saddened Gennady Smakov in his book *The Great Russian Dancers* (published by Knopf in 1984), "seems to relate more to psychological needs of the moment than to the dubious artistic results." On the TV special *Baryshnikov in Hollywood,* Smakov's sarcasm turned to bile: "The vapidity . . . could challenge the silliness of the most nonsensical soap opera."

Few of his associates—Charles France being the notable exception—have understood the intensity of Baryshnikov's desire to be a popular entertainer. "It seems," the dancer said, "that some people find it very vulgar whenever I depart from the ballet stage. I must agree. Very vulgar. But, you know, I love the intensity and the energy popular entertainers have in America. I feel this same thing inside me, and I don't think it is such a bad thing to shock some people sometime. For much of my life, you know, I have had to live with other people's ideas of what is the appropriate thing for me to do. I find that the moment people have come up with a verdict is exactly the same time I want to change the whole scene. I am me, not what someone else thinks is me."

Where does this penchant leave American Ballet Theatre? Probably without Baryshnikov as artistic director at some point, and probably sooner rather than later. If he lingers, it is not for love of the job but for love of the people who come with it. His ambivalence toward many aspects of the role the administration and board expect him to play is manifested over and over again, and there are times when the emotional and practical demands of the dancers are clearly oppressive. He lingers with the company out of loyalty and affection, and also because of a certain insecurity about which direction, exactly, he should be charging off toward. The goal of creating an American Ballet Theatre that is recognized for the brilliance and distinctiveness of its style and the range of its repertoire is very important to him, but at some point he is going to decide that he has done what he is capable of doing, and then he will be gone.

Late one afternoon during the company's season at the Metropolitan Opera House, where his company's production of *The Sleeping Beauty* was playing to sold-out audiences day after day, Baryshnikov walked the short distance across the central plaza at Lincoln Center to the New York State Theater to take part in a very special event staged by ABT's great rival, the New York City Ballet. Lincoln Kirstein, the illustrious and sustaining animator of City Ballet, had turned eighty and the company was staging a birthday party for him in front of a full house. The magnitude of Kirstein's contribution to dance in America and the lofty position he had reached— long before his ninth decade on earth was trumpeted at this stylish party—can scarcely be overestimated. It wasn't simply that he was the man who brought Balanchine to America and set him loose; Kirstein redirected his entire life to fulfill one great cause—the establishment of an American tradition in dance wedded to one man's choreographic genius. Although married, Kirstein made Balanchine, and the company that the two men created, a sort of family. Wealthy, he contributed most of his private fortune to the cause. Critical, he transformed one of the most original and probing analytical minds of this century—his own—into an eclectic and wholly effective propaganda machine to further Balanchinian classicism. He created the School of American Ballet to give his cause authority and durability. He hustled sustaining funds for City Ballet with a degree of sophistication and strong-arm tactics that made Larry Lynn seem like a novice at a nunnery. And all of it directed toward the vision of Mr. B.

At eighty, Lincoln Kirstein was still full of life, cantankerous as ever, still capable of making trouble, and showing hardly a trace of the mellowness that allegedly overtakes even the crustiest of old troupers. At his birthday party—which one wag in the audience, perhaps thinking of what happened to ABT's Princess Aurora each night over at the Met, called "The Apotheosis of Lincoln"—the opening tribute was a Balanchine ballet: respectful, appropriate, and predictable. Then the whole affair came gloriously unstuck. Peter Martins, the amiable Danish dancer saddled with the unenviable challenge of succeeding Balanchine (and getting through the day with the often irascible Kirstein), emerged on center stage to announce that the company's birthday present to its Grand Old

Man was a production of . . . *The Sleeping Beauty.* It had been Balanchine's wish, Martins said, to pay tribute to the memories of his own youth—just as Diaghilev had done when he remounted *The Sleeping Princess* in London in 1921—with a revival of the greatest of the Imperial ballets. City Ballet's production, Martins promised, would incorporate choreography Balanchine had already created before he died. Who was to work out the rest of the evening choreographically was sensibly left vague.

A buzz went around the hall. *The Sleeping Beauty* was not the kind of production loyal City Ballet fans expected to see from their company. This was the sort of overblown stuff Ballet Theatre did all the time. This *was* the very ballet ABT was performing at the moment. As this buzzing went around, the curtain went up to reveal . . . Mikhail Baryshnikov. As a tribute to Kirstein, the artistic director of City Ballet's great rival had happily agreed to take on the role of Ringmaster in Jerome Robbins's charming *divertissement* for two dozen little girls, called *Circus Polka*. It was not a demanding role: Baryshnikov was simply required to flick a whip in the air every now and then, and the little girls—all from Kirstein's School of American Ballet—went through their well-rehearsed paces.

At the end, Lincoln Kirstein was inevitably enticed onto the stage. He thanked everyone most profusely and then moved a little off from the center to acknowledge the applause of the audience. On his right were the two youthful artistic directors of America's best ballet companies. He smiled at both and gave them a short, courtly bow. The audience roared its approval, and for the first time Kirstein beamed. After a few moments he turned slightly to his right and moved toward the two men. Peter Martins, the official host of the celebration, seemed vaguely perplexed as to what to do next, but not Kirstein. Still beaming, he moved closer to Mikhail Baryshnikov and put his arm around his shoulder. It was clearly a spontaneous and natural instinct, heightened by the euphoria of the occasion. It was also an exceedingly provocative sight. Side by side, there was Lincoln Kirstein and the latest Mr. B. . . .

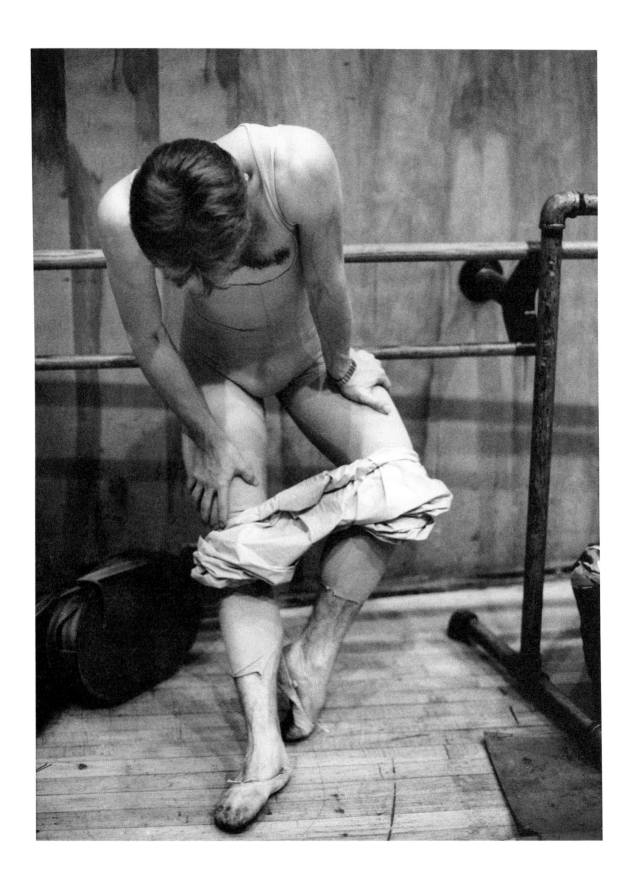

JOHAN RENVALL

EPILOGUE

*B*y the end of the 1986–1987 season, Susan Jaffe was "feeling good—in my body and in my mind." She was getting back into shape after being forced to give up all her roles during ABT's long sojourn at the Met in New York, and there was a special ferocity in her high energy level during rehearsals. Or at least there was until she slipped and flipped on her side during a rehearsal in Washington, D.C., a slip which fortunately resulted in only a minor injury.

Jaffe refused to get superstitious. Within a few days she was working at full tilt again and flew off to Denmark with the company for a major television taping. Everything was going well until five minutes before she was supposed to go before the cameras for the first taping session. She bent down in her dressing room and banged her knee against a sharp metallic point beneath a sink. The resulting gash, which split her knee open, required a dozen stitches. All her roles for the taping were reassigned, and finally, at this point, she became very superstitious.

"I'd really had it by then," Jaffe said. "I thought something or someone was out there doing very bad things to me. I was beside myself." By the spring of 1988, having made it through eight injury-free months, superstitions were receding. She was dancing all over America and waiting—once again—for the Met season to begin.

At the tag end of 1987, on Tuesday, December 29, shortly after noon, Patrick Bissell was found dead in his apartment in Hoboken, New Jersey, by his current girlfriend, Amy Rose. She had returned from dancing in *The Nutcracker* with American Ballet Theatre in Los Angeles the day before and had gone to his apartment that night. There had been no answer. Concerned, she returned late the next morning and got a key from the building superintendent. Entering the apartment, Rose found Bissell reclining on the couch, fully clothed. He may have been dead for a couple of days.

A few hours later Charles Dillingham telephoned Mikhail Baryshnikov at his home. "I have some very bad news," he told the artistic director. "Patrick is dead."

Baryshnikov's initial reaction was that it was a black joke. Then he remembered whom he was talking to, and the realization that this was fact left him with a queasy feeling in his stomach.

"I had been talking to Patrick several days before," he recalled later. "You know, he hadn't signed a contract yet, but he was turning up for class, and I said to him we would get together when he felt fully up to shape. He smiled. You know that guy had a big, big smile."

Charles France heard the news from ABT's associate publicity director, Elena Gordon, and he, too, took it very hard. Perhaps more than anyone in the company, he had been agonizing over Bissell's chaotic life almost from the beginning. The dancer's arrival at American Ballet Theatre nearly fifteen years earlier coincided with France's own rise within the hierarchy.

"He was a favorite dancer of mine, and I say that knowing Patrick Bissell was always one really difficult person to handle. He had a terrible temper and he could be very scheming. But he also had enormous charm. He just loved women and he was always very courtly around them. He could be very vain and boastful, but he was also weirdly modest. His consideration for his female partners was often extremely moving. He wanted his women to look beautiful when they were dancing. Ballet was this great starry fantasy for him and it meant a great deal to him to have an important role in making that fantasy a reality. Of course there was this other side, this very destructive side. We know all about that now, but we didn't know anything about the psychological torment of his childhood. Perhaps if we did we might have understood him better. Still, I would like it understood that there were people inside Ballet Theatre who knew he was a very loving person who needed and got a lot of love in return."

It was also true, as dancers within the company would openly argue, that as much—if not more—attention was paid to the "Patrick Bissell problem" than any other. Both Baryshnikov and France admit the truth of the charge, if charge it is. In a large company like ABT, it is very difficult—if not impossible—for the senior staff to have an intimate relationship with a dancer. The nature of day-to-day professionalism almost prohibits it, even if there were time to spend more than a few minutes on any single problem. With troublesome dancers, however, this scenario changes dramatically. The nature of the trouble gets caught up in the proper functioning of the company. Bissell was a very special case, because his talent and potential were the equal of his penchant for causing chaos. He was certainly the proverbial black sheep, twice fired and thrice hired. Even at the best of times it was in his nature to draw attention to himself, and because he had an exceptional talent, the artistic staff was always trying to work things out—some way, somehow. "It's a little difficult, and perhaps a bit too personal, to explain this business adequately," said Charles France, "but the life of people on the artistic staff is rather lonely. It is certainly independent of the dancers' lives—who often have one another to console each other—but artistic staff members are usually independent of each other as well. The reality is that the amount of time spent by a lot of us on Patrick's problems meant that we felt very close to him, and that he had become strangely important in our lives. For me personally, his death left a void of both confrontation and contact. Despite all the difficulties, he had become someone who mattered a very great deal to me. His death hit us all very hard."

It hit even harder after the news had been picked up by the media. Coverage ranged from the elegiac to the predictably sensational. The banner headline on the front page of the *New York Post* read BALLET STAR FOUND DEAD. Below the two-inch type was the human-interest element under the headline: "Hooked on coke since 14." The *Post* quoted Bissell's distraught mother, Patricia Bissell, in a general indictment of the ballet ambience: "I've been backstage," Mrs. Bissell was reported saying. "I've seen the Kleenex boxes and cocaine noses." This statement left many dancers at ABT mystified because they could not recall ever having seen Mrs. Bissell backstage at any of the company's rehearsals or performances. The statement had to be denied officially, adding to the general aura of tortured grief.

Within another day, Gelsey Kirkland also entered the fray. Bissell had introduced Kirkland to the higher mysteries of hard drugs, and although she announced that she had kicked the habit and purged herself emotionally with the publication of her book, giving all the details of her nightmare, she still had scores to settle. She tried—somewhat disingenuously, it appeared to some—to hold American Ballet Theatre responsible for the death.

Hindsight can often be brutal and hypocritical. In the sad tale of

Patrick Bissell, hindsight showed death to be the logical consequence of a life-style that moved on the fast track without much thought given to brakes. Short of a mother's complicated grief (Mrs. Bissell gave *People* magazine an account of how she repeatedly beat her son as a child and told him: "I don't want to be your mother"), people in and out of the company who knew Bissell well were initially numbed by the awful inevitability of it all. After a time, they focused their thoughts, and their statements and observations eventually restored to Bissell a measure of dignity in death that his talent deserved.

Before this balm of friendship and respect could begin to take effect among the company, American Ballet Theatre was briefly thrown back into the vortex of scandal and notoriety, with the accusations of both Mrs. Bissell and Kirkland left hanging in the air. Baryshnikov made a dignified reply, but the myth of a drug-besotted company was too enticing to some in the media to leave alone. It was not that the charges of drug use in ballet companies were unfounded, but that the comprehensive accusations, based on fabrication, were unfair. Professional dance is a stressful business, and as in any number of stressful professions, there will always be some who are tempted to deal with the stress with drugs. In a tight-knit, high-pressure touring troupe like ABT, however, it is simply untrue that dancers can disguise a serious addiction. At Ballet Theatre, there have been only two cases of dancers' trying to carry on as usual with serious addictions: Patrick Bissell and Gelsey Kirkland. And they both had to be fired to bring them to an adult awareness of their problem.

In Bissell's case, this evidently did not work, for he was dead at thirty. That was a fact. He had been hooked since he was a young teenager, and that was a fact too. People at American Ballet Theatre may not have done everything they could have done to save him, but only in the sense that no one can do everything to save someone who cannot save himself. Susan Jones, the régisseur, cared about him; Charles France cared deeply for him; Mikhail Baryshnikov did him the honor of rising to righteous anger whenever he saw evidence of the addiction, an anger that was transformed into practical help, emotional support, and financial assistance for Bissell's stays at the Betty Ford Clinic. None of this, alone or cumulatively, was sufficient. That is a fact. In the end, Patrick Bissell played a final and bitter role as a cautionary symbol for all who flirt with and then embrace induced illusions. It is a cruel verdict, but inescapable.

*   *   *

Having vowed to end his active dancing days soon, having admonished anyone in the higher echelons of ABT who tried to get him dancing on the company's own stages, having complained bitterly that his body can't take it anymore, having darkly hinted in Bari, Italy, that he might never dance Albrecht in *Giselle* again, Mikhail Baryshnikov found himself in San Francisco in 1988 with five Giselles but—thanks to another spate of injuries—only two beleaguered and overworked Albrechts. His ankle injury the previous summer turned out to be not as bad as was initially feared. And so, swearing sarcastically at fate, Baryshnikov was preparing to dance in two performances of *Giselle.*

"It will be okay," he said. "You know, an old dog can still jump for a bone. I'm forty now. Any day I am going to wake up and my brain will finally catch up to my body and a lot of people are going to hear me scream *'Aaaaargh.'* But tomorrow? Tomorrow I dance Albrecht."

BALLET THEATRE FOUNDATION, INC.
presents

American Ballet Theatre 1988

Richard Pleasant
Founder
1940

Lucia Chase Oliver Smith
Directors
1945-1980

Antony Tudor
1908-1987
Choreographer Emeritus

Artistic Director
Mikhail Baryshnikov

Artistic Associate
Sir Kenneth MacMillan

Associate Director
John Taras

**Victor Barbee Julio Bocca Leslie Browne
Alessandra Ferri Cynthia Gregory Susan Jaffe
Kevin McKenzie Amanda McKerrow Michael Owen Johan Renvall
Ross Stretton Marianna Tcherkassky Clark Tippet
Martine van Hamel Cheryl Yeager**

Cynthia Anderson Ethan Brown Ricardo Bustamante Deirdre Carberry
Wes Chapman Christine Dunham John Gardner Robert Hill
Lucette Katerndahl Bonnie Moore Kathleen Moore Amy Rose Christine Spizzo

Anne Adair Deanne Albert Claudia Alfieri Melissa Allen Charles Askegard
Antonia Berasaluce Shawn Black Gabrielle Brown Sandra Brown Elizabeth Carr
Karen Christensen Jeremy Collins David Cuevas Elizabeth Dunn Cristina Escoda
Christina Fagundes Paul Faria Elizabeth Ferrell Roman Greller Amy Groos
Mark Grothman Alice Heeley Careen Hobart Laura Hood Eileen Houghton Lorin Johnson
Carld Jonassaint Julie Kent John Wey Ling Veronica Lynn Marie-France
Christopher Martin Christopher Mattox Geoffrey Moore Rachel Moore Rosalie O'Connor
Isabella Padovani Keith Roberts Hilary Ryan Scott Schlexer Loren Schmalle
Raymond Serrano Dana Stackpole Lillie Stewart William Stolar Bettina Sulser
John Summers Thomas Terry Thomas Titone Ashley Tuttle Roger van Fleteren
Greet Vinckier Robert Wallace AliceAnn Wilson Mary Wilson
Craig Wright Ross Yearsley Jennet Zerbe

Assistant to the Artistic Director
Charles France

Principal Conductor
Jack Everly

Régisseur
Susan Jones

*Ballet Mistress for the
Classical Repertoire*
Elena Tchernichova

Conductors
Charles Barker
Emil de Cou

Ballet Mistresses
Georgina Parkinson
Wendy Walker
Ballet Masters
Michael Lland
Jurgen Schneider
Terence S. Orr
David Richardson